LEARNING TO
LOVE
M÷TH

Also by
Judy Willis

Research-Based Strategies to Ignite Student Learning
Brain-Friendly Strategies for the Inclusion Classroom
Teaching the Brain to Read: Strategies for Improving Fluency, Vocabulary,
*   and Comprehension*

LEARNING TO
LOVE
MATH

TEACHING **STRATEGIES** THAT CHANGE STUDENT ATTITUDES AND GET RESULTS

JUDY WILLIS, M.D.

ASCD | Alexandria, Virginia

1703 N. Beauregard St. • Alexandria, VA 22311-1714 USA
Phone: 800-933-2723 or 703-578-9600 • Fax: 703-575-5400
Web site: www.ascd.org • E-mail: member@ascd.org
Author guidelines: www.ascd.org/write

Gene R. Carter, *Executive Director;* Judy Zimny, *Chief Program Development Officer;* Nancy Modrak, *Publisher;* Scott Willis, *Director, Book Acquisitions & Development;* Julie Houtz, *Director, Book Editing & Production;* Jamie Greene, *Editor;* Sima Nasr, *Senior Graphic Designer;* Mike Kalyan, *Production Manager;* Carmen Yuhas, *Production Specialist;* Circle Graphics, *Desktop Publishing Specialist*

All Web links in this book are correct as of the publication date below but may have become inactive or otherwise modified since that time. If you notice a deactivated or changed link, please e-mail books@ascd.org with the words "Link Update" in the subject line. In your message, please specify the Web link, the book title, and the page number on which the link appears.

PAPERBACK ISBN: 978-1-4166-1036-6   ASCD product #108073   n7/10
Also available as an e-book (see Books in Print for the ISBNs).

Quantity discounts for the paperback edition only: 10–49 copies, 10%; 50+ copies, 15%; for 1,000 or more copies, call 800-933-2723, ext. 5634, or 703-575-5634. For desk copies: member@ascd.org.

Library of Congress Cataloging-in-Publication Data
Willis, Judy.
   Learning to love math : teaching strategies that change student attitudes and get results / Judy Willis.
      p. cm.
   Includes bibliographical references and index.
   ISBN 978-1-4166-1036-6 (pbk. : alk. paper) 1. Mathematics—Study and teaching—Psychological aspects. I. Title.
   QA11.2.W58 2010
   510.71—dc22
                                                                                            2010014053

20 19 18 17 16   6 7 8 9 10 11 12

Dedicated to the BRAIN, because you are not stubborn or stuck in your ways. Your generous plasticity lets your owners determine their own intelligence.

LEARNING TO LOVE MATH

Acknowledgments

Much appreciation goes to my editor, Jamie Greene, without whose suggestions both the structure and readability of this book would have been much less coherent. To Scott Willis and the team in book acquisitions: no matter what I needed, even though it may have had nothing to do with book acquisitions, Scott never said, "That's not my department." His positive attitude must keep his amygdala wide open and dopamine up enough to give transfusions.

Tim Ito is the Internet technology guru with a zero nerd factor. He is such a visionary and so considerate that I can never say *no* to any of his requests. Although it was never my plan to do any blogging, tweeting, or Facebooking, Tim walked me over the threshold, and I happily found a wonderland where I once imagined ogres. I am also grateful to Simon Cable, who read this book with such focus and comprehension that he created my online author interview, which distills the book's most important concepts into tantalizing invitations for others to try the offered neuro-*logical* strategies.

Jay McTighe has my highest respect as an educational visionary with the practical strategies to empower educators and academic policymakers with the courage to uplift even the most curriculum-burdened units of instruction and go beyond "covering" standards to "uncovering" durable knowledge. He has guided—and continues to guide—educators and administrators worldwide who admire and appreciate the logic of his approach and clarity with which he presents and writes about planning and teaching students. The information Jay shares enables educators to effectively change students' brains from being temporary resting places for isolated facts into active processing tools where concepts are born, are enriched, and become the tools of wisdom that students take with them far beyond the test and classroom walls. I am honored and grateful for Jay's friendship, guidance, and generosity. His tutelage has opened doors in my own brain, and his efforts on my behalf continue to extend the scope and reach available for me to share my information with educators. I give Jay the Lifetime *Mensch* Award.

I am grateful to Dawson and all my math students these past five years at Santa Barbara Middle School. Five years after Dawson was in my 7th grade algebra class, his mom sent me his college application letter. It contained the reinforcement that keeps us all teaching despite ever-increasing reasons for math negativity in our students. Dawson wrote, "My seventh grade math teacher, Dr. Judy Willis, a neuroscientist turned math teacher, was the first teacher to understand my brain and work with me to make it work for me. I started to see my mind as an asset of which to be proud instead of a detriment to my learning." What would we educators do without those students who give us their trust and persevere through challenge? Because we believe in them, they believe in us, and we change lives.

Of course, much love and gratitude is due to my husband Paul, who never pressures me to limit my speaking engagements or step away from my research journals and computer but gently tempts me with a glass of wine and an invitation to see a great sunset. Paul generously understands when I need to drive my own car to dinners with friends so I can leave before dessert if I start to obsess about rewriting a chapter for the fifth time or revising a presentation that was fine even before its third edit. I am so fortunate to be married to my college sweetheart.

I love and honor my mother, Norma Allerhand, who never "got" math, but never negated its value. She encouraged her children with the assurance that we were more than the sum of our genetic pool and could reach our own heights in math and all endeavors. I appreciate the wisdom I learned from Malana and Alani, my daughters. They helped me relate to parents who said their children eschewed their help with math because they didn't do it "the way the teacher does." My girls eventually trained me to understand that my support and confidence in them was more valuable than my hovering.

Introduction

....

> Human history becomes more and more a race between education and catastrophe.
>
> —H. G. Wells

No other school subject pushes emotional buttons the way math does. It usually falls at the bottom of a list of subjects that people like or in which they feel interested or successful. Yet it's increasingly clear that building an education system that provides students with a strong foundation in math is important for both individuals and society.

From a broad perspective, today's world presents us with an increasing volume of information (from online sources, for example) that is not pre-filtered for accuracy or evaluated for all potential uses. Under these circumstances, the ability to make sound personal, financial, political, ethical, and social decisions requires mathematical thinking, careful observations, and sound deductions. These skills, in turn, utilize information that the brain validates and interprets using developed reasoning skills.

More specifically, a well-educated workforce is needed to handle increasingly complex technology. It is obvious that the people who employ auto mechanics or plumbers aren't looking for candidates with limited math knowledge to work on their customers' expensive cars or water filtration systems, no matter what technical skills those candidates might have. As the future quickly becomes the present, it is becoming clear that almost all professions (with human employees) will require some degree of mathematical thinking. Quite simply, this is because unpredictable problems inevitably arise for which creative solutions are required. Machines and computers don't possess the transferable conceptual knowledge required to address these problems. Reassuringly, it is for this reason that jobs will always be available for people—as long as they have the foundational knowledge, conceptual understanding, and executive functions of the human brain's prefrontal cortex (PFC).

Mathematical thinking is a perfect example of the higher-order thinking that is unique to the prefrontal cortex. The executive functions of the PFC—including personal responsibility, emotional response control, planning, prioritizing, gratification delay, organization, creative problem solving, critical analysis, judgment, prediction, and self-motivation—are exactly the skills that 21st-century employers look for. They also represent what our globalized society requires in order to solve a wide array of problems—both known and unknown. Though these executive functions are, most likely, still nascent in your students, your guidance and experiences will help your students recognize the inherent link between effort and progress and ultimately help them develop these necessary functions.

Students with mathematical competence also have other critical abilities, such as reasoning, abstraction, pattern and relationship recognition, and conceptual thinking—skills needed to use and apply knowledge in a variety of contexts (U.S. Department of Education, 2008). The processes used in logical-mathematical thinking—categorization, classification, inference, generalization, calculation, and hypothesis testing—are the foundations of higher-order thinking skills that transfer to other subjects beyond mathematics. These executive functions provide today's students with opportunities to be tomorrow's creative problem solvers. With these abilities, our students can charge into the 21st century with more preparation and confidence.

Moving from Negative to Positive

Too often, students have a negative attitude toward learning math. You can take steps to reverse that attitude. You can provide students with opportunities to develop personal connections to math so they value the acquisition of math knowledge. Neuroscience research reveals a connection between enjoyable, participatory learning and long-term memory. Students work harder and persevere through challenges when they have concrete personal goals and motivation for mastering the subject knowledge. With interest and lasting memory, your students can learn math with a depth of comprehension that extends beyond the test—and even beyond summer vacation. Interventions that can help students overcome their negative attitudes include the following:

- Evaluating and planning so that each student works at an individually appropriate level of *achievable challenge.*
- Building missing foundation skills through strategies such as "errorless math," prediction and estimating, and scaffolding with cue words, previews, and calculators.
- Teaching to students' strengths and with their interests in mind.
- Recognizing the link between effort and goal achievement.
- Using strategies to reduce negative responses to mistakes (e.g., modeling appropriate reactions, discussing common mistakes and how to avoid them) and increase levels of participation.

We'll explore each of these interventions in the following chapters, but the concept of *achievable challenge* is an important underlying principle that is worth emphasizing here. Indeed, a central goal of this book is to show you how to differentiate for each student's level of achievable challenge. No two classes have students with the same learning strengths, cultural influences, special needs, foundational skills, and conceptual levels in math numeracy, language, or reading abilities. Sometimes students come to our classrooms from schools with less successful math instruction or schools that use different instructional systems. Teachers who use strategies to differentiate and adapt the curriculum according to the foundational knowledge of their students increase the likelihood of successfully meeting those students' varying needs. However, professional development and mentoring that target new curriculum content sometimes fall short. To fill this gap, I'll describe how to evaluate each student's achievable challenge level relative to each new unit so instruction can be applied appropriately to lower the barriers, not the bar.

A Note About "Gray Matter"

I find that when the educators I work with in professional development programs and workshops discover how the brain transforms sensory data into bits of knowledge, they share a common reaction. Their "aha!" moment comes from knowing *why* one's best lessons are so successful. Because they can connect their teaching success to an understanding of which neural systems were engaged at maximal efficiency (i.e., what happened in their students' brains during lessons when everything went well), these teachers have gone on to modify their less successful lessons and collaborate with colleagues on new lessons using brain-based research as a guide.

The "Gray Matter" sections in this book provide background to help you gain knowledge about brain structure and function so that you can better understand your students' learning strengths and needs. Knowing why a strategy is neuro-*logical* lets you modify it to suit the needs of different students and curricula. When you know why a strategy works, you become more confident and invested in it. Your students will perceive your confidence and enthusiasm, and these perceptions will help them replace their own math negativity with math confidence.

As you share what you learn about the brain with your students, they will undoubtedly clamor to know more about how their own brains work and how they can increase their intelligence. Like you, your students can be empowered by the insights that come from understanding why and how particular strategies work. Students are typically more receptive to assignments when they have specific tools at hand (see Appendix B, Brain Owner's Manual). They will understand that their brains build stronger, more efficient neural networks and store longer memories when they estimate, solve math problems in more than one way, and apply math beyond the classroom. You and your students will even find an answer to the common question, "Why do we have to learn this?" The answer: "Because it makes our brains grow and we become smarter!"

Reversing Math Negativity
with an Attitude Makeover

> I let that negativity roll off me like water off a duck's back. If it's not
> positive, I didn't hear it. If you can overcome the negativity, everything
> becomes easier.
>
> —George Foreman

The first step to success in math is a positive attitude. Yet that's the last thing
we can expect from many of our students.

Many students, like their parents before them, come to our classrooms with valid feelings that make them unhappy doing math. A 2005
AP-AOL News poll of 1,000 adults in the United States revealed that
37 percent recalled that they "hated" math in school. In the poll, more than
twice as many people said they hated math as said they hated any other
subject. (The poll was conducted by Ipsos, an international polling firm,
and has a margin-of-sampling error of plus or minus 3 percentage points.)

One would think that once they were out of school, these folks would
have found the real-world value of the math they disdained in school. In an
evaluation of math literacy of a random sampling of adults in the United
States, 71 percent could not calculate miles per gallon on a trip, and 58
percent were unable to calculate a 10 percent tip for a lunch bill. Yet only
15 percent of those polled said they wished that they had learned more
about or studied more math in school (Phillips, 2007).

Myths and misconceptions about math abound, such as the following:

- You have to be very intelligent to be good at math.
- It is acceptable to be bad at math because most people are.
- Math isn't really used much outside of special occupations.

In addition, many people have the attitude, "My parents said they were never good at math, so they don't expect me to be any different."

Why is there so much negativity about math? Causes include low self-expectations as a result of past experiences with math, parental bias against math, inadequate skills to succeed at math learning, failure to engage math through learning strengths, and fear of making mistakes. As teachers know all too well, math negativity has various consequences. These include stress, low motivation, decreased levels of participation, boredom,

GRAY MATTER

Parental Influence

Many parents of today's students learned math by doing worksheets and drills, and they expect the same for their children. Parents who were successful in math through repeated memorization skills (rather than strong concept development) may resent alternative math instruction, such as inquiry and manipulatives, for their children. A possible result is that some parents may feel frustrated when they can't help their children with the unfamiliar homework.

However, it is likely that their children don't share these parents' verbal, linguistic, and auditory learning strengths. The top three intelligences found among students today are linguistic, visual-spatial, and tactile-kinesthetic. These are the same intelligences that characterized most learners 25 years ago, but the percentage of students in each category has changed. The proportion of linguistic (auditory) learners has dropped, and there is a greater preponderance of visual learners. Visual-spatial learners now account for more than 50 percent of students, 35 percent are tactile-kinesthetic, and only 15 percent are linguistic learners (Gardner, 2000).

low tolerance for challenge, failure to keep pace with class lessons, behavior problems, and avoidance of the advanced math classes necessary for subsequent professional success.

Getting Students Back in the Picture

In a study that looked at middle school students' perceptions of academic engagement (Bishop & Pflaum, 2005), 5th and 6th graders were asked to draw their *typical* learning experiences and then draw learning experiences they *liked*. In the drawings of typical experiences, teachers and chalkboards were the focus, and the students usually did not include themselves in the picture. In the drawings of learning they liked, the students featured themselves prominently.

This finding is especially pertinent to math negativity. Consider the frustration that results when children learn math by memorizing facts and procedures instead of building on a firm understanding of concepts. Long division, for example, is an early math challenge, usually taught as a procedure to be memorized and incorporating subtraction, addition, and multiplication—often before these preliminary skills have been fully mastered. Therefore, children typically struggle to solve long-division problems with remainders (e.g., $67 \div 8 = 8$ with a remainder of 3). Solving these problems is usually not very pleasant for students, but by the time they have completed enough drills and built the mathematical foundation necessary to succeed (usually around 5th or 6th grade), they are inexplicably asked to report quotients with decimals or fractions, not remainders. Textbooks and teachers alternately ask students to round the answer to the nearest tenth, round to the nearest hundredth, express the answer in fraction form with mixed numbers, or express it in fraction form with improper fractions.

Students are usually not told *why* they must make these changes. If they are given reasons, the reasons are often confusing or vague. I recall that the first time I assigned textbook homework that asked for answers to be given in different formats, I did not have a clear rationale for my 5th grade students. No explanation is given for which representation of the answer is best, nor is one provided for when the different variations should be reported; yet the demands to answer questions in these varying formats continually appears on homework and tests. In many schools, children don't have the opportunity to participate in classroom discussions about the real-world implications—that can actually be significant—of remainders or decimals.

For example, when it comes to the rate of interest on large sums of money, the difference between 8.3 and 8.375 percent can matter to the borrower. Other times, decimal or remainder answers might be inconsequential, such as figuring how many eight-person tables are needed to seat 67 children at a pizza party. Whether the remainder is 3 or the decimal part of the quotient is .375 does not make any real difference because *any* remainder or decimal means that an entire additional table is needed.

In this light, why *wouldn't* students develop math negativity, frustration, and stress? They are routinely asked to memorize procedures and are then told—without explanation or conceptual connections—that what was correct last year is no longer acceptable. The curriculum rarely primes their interest with opportunities to *want* to know how to represent remainders in different forms. Without clearly evident personal value, the brain—operating at the level of information intake and memory formation—doesn't care.

Students truly "get" math when they see it applied in real-life ways they care about—in other words, when they see math as a tool they need and want. This motivation is not promoted in word problems about the number of books or the number of students in a classroom. However, when you give small groups of students 67 toothpicks and some index cards and then ask them to model the pizza party seating problem described earlier, they'll build the experiential knowledge of a real-world situation where remainders are not helpful. When they consider dividing leftover pieces of pizza into parts, they will see that fractions or decimals are a valuable tool to make the pizza sharing process fair, whereas a "remainder" would imply that perfectly good pieces of pizza sit in the box because there is no way to divide them.

Most elementary arithmetic skills are "learned" by rote memorization and assessed on tests of memory recall. Children who do not excel at memorizing isolated facts are less successful, feel inadequate, and lose confidence in their ability to do math. The result is a cascade of increased math anxiety, lowered self-confidence, alienation, and failure. This is a pity because the ability to memorize basic arithmetic and multiplication tables does not determine who lives up to their math potential. With this goal in mind, the ability to recognize patterns and construct mental concepts that use foundational math facts is far more valuable.

Math that is "taught to the tests" has a negative effect even on the children who succeed with this approach. The problem is not that they won't rise to standardized-test expectations; they *will,* but their achievement will stop there. If your math curriculum doesn't include problems that students *want* to solve and discussions that connect those problems to what students *need* to learn, your intervention is critical to prevent increasing student ambivalence to and alienation from math.

Building Math Positivity

Before children can become interested in math, they have to be comfortable with it. They must perceive their environment as physically and psychologically safe before learning can occur. Students build resilience and coping strategies when they learn how to use their academic strengths to build math skills and strategies. Your intervention helps them strengthen the networks that carry information through their brains' emotional filters to the area where higher-order thinking skills are concentrated, the prefrontal cortex (PFC). With practice, they will be able to use the highest-level analytical networks in the PFC to evaluate incoming information and discover creative solutions to math problems (in addition to problems in all subject areas). To better understand how your students learn, it is important to first learn how to propel information through those filters and begin building math positivity.

✤ STRATEGY: Arrange Family Conferences

No one wants to add to student pressure, especially when you suspect that a student will suffer emotional or even physical abuse if he or she does not meet certain parental expectations in math. Parents with extremely high expectations for their children are usually motivated by a desire to see their children have more than they have themselves. Unfortunately, when children

GRAY MATTER

The Amygdala as Stress Filter

Reversing negative attitudes toward math may take months if your students have been repeatedly stressed to the point of feeling helpless and hopeless. If your students are anxious during math class, information entering their brains is less likely to reach the conscious thinking and long-term memory parts of the prefrontal cortex, and learning will not take place. Stress is the primary filter blocker that needs to be overcome. Perception of a real or imagined threat creates stress, as does the *frustration* of confusion or the *boredom* of repetition.

Stress blocks the flow of information through the amygdala in the brain's limbic system (i.e., the part that controls emotion) to the PFC, and it diverts sensory input into the automatic, reflexive parts of the lower brain. These are the unconscious, more primitive brain networks that prepare the body to react to potential danger, where the only possible responses are fight, flight, or freeze. Under stressful conditions, emotion is dominant over cognition, and the rational-thinking PFC has limited influence on behavior, focus, memory, and problem solving (Kienast et al., 2008). Prior negative experiences also impede the flow (through the amygdala) of stored memories needed to understand new, related information and to use foundational knowledge to solve new problems (LeDoux, 1994).

The implications of stress-related thinking and memory problems are beginning to be understood at the neural level, where emotions enhance or impair cognition and learning (Goleman, 1995). When students are stressed, they can't use their thinking brains. Therefore, a reduction in math-related stress is key to success.

internalize these expectations and don't fulfill them, they can suffer depression, anxiety, physical illnesses (high levels of cortisol associated with chronic stress lowers the immune response), or psychosomatic illnesses, or they may even inflict physical injury on themselves and others.

Family conferences can help parents learn some of the scientific evidence linking the effects of stress to academic success. These interventions will also allow you to explain that the first step to math success is a positive attitude toward the subject matter, not just to the grades associated with it.

You can also suggest ways for these parents to be involved in a positive way. Explain that the brain is most receptive to learning about a topic when there is a clear link between that topic and something the child values. Parents can act as "math allies" if they find ways to integrate real-world math into their child's hobbies and interests. For example, they can encourage their children to calculate how long it will be until their special television show begins if it is currently 3:00 and the show starts at 5:30. They can also help their children compare the costs of things they like (e.g., bicycles, toys, computers) in newspaper ads that offer various percentage discounts off different base prices.

✤ STRATEGY: Retest to De-stress

Reassure all students that if they want to achieve high grades, they will have opportunities that will allow them to regain some sense of control, such as retests. Because progress in math is so strongly based on foundational knowledge, students need to achieve mastery in each topic—which forms the basis from which students can extend their neural networks of patterns and concepts—before they move to the next level. Retests provide opportunities to reevaluate answers and make corrections, as necessary. To ensure mastery, I require that students take a retest when they score under 85 percent. My primary goal is to have students learn the appropriate material so they can move forward with an adequate background for success.

Incorporating accountability into retesting allows students to build skills related to self-reliance, goal planning, and independent learning. Parents or colleagues may voice concerns that students might not act responsibly or seriously once they realize that they'll have a second chance. Accountability increases when you require students to provide evidence of corrective action, such as participating in tutoring, doing skill reviews, or finding textual examples that correctly demonstrate how the type of problem is solved. If the original test and retest scores are averaged together, students understand that they remain accountable for that first test grade.

Compared with cheating (an unfortunate response to grade pressure that further decreases confidence and self-esteem), the option of taking retests is a more positive approach to low grades. Retesting takes time on your part, but it shows your students that you respect their capacity to be responsible, successful learners.

♣ STRATEGY: Demonstrate the Value of Math

Key to developing students' interest in math is to capture their imaginations. Instead of allowing them to think of math as an isolated subject, show the extended values of math in ways they find inspiring. If you teach elementary school, find opportunities throughout the day to show students the ways they benefit from mathematics and how it is applicable to their areas of interest. For example, students can use math to determine the number of absent students by counting the students present and then "counting back" to subtract.

In upper grades, cross-curricular planning is a way to achieve this goal. Older students, for example, can solve meaningful problems related to the

GRAY MATTER

How a Positive Attitude Enhances Problem Solving

Solving problems with insight is a function of the anterior cingulated cortex (ACC) within the prefrontal cortex. The ACC also allocates attention resources and modulates motivation. Functional magnetic resonance imaging (fMRI) scans show increased metabolic activity in this region when subjects think about how to solve a problem. A recent study (Subramaniam, Kounios, Bowden, Parrish, & Jung-Beeman, 2009) showed that even before the subjects realized the answer, the ACC showed increased activation, predicting their subsequent awareness of the insight. Positive emotional states increased greater baseline activity in the ACC and were associated with more successful problem solving.

A related study (Fredrickson, Tugade, Waugh, & Larkin, 2003) demonstrated expanded peripheral vision during positive emotional states and more creative problem solving. Negative emotions, on the other hand, narrowed peripheral vision and appeared to similarly limit insight.

quantity and price of tickets they need to sell in order to cover their expenses for an upcoming field trip. When you increase your students' positive feelings toward mathematics, you unlock their brains' math-blocking filters, promote long-term memory, and foster greater understanding beyond rote memorization.

✤ STRATEGY: Start the Year Showing That You Care

To demonstrate interest in your students as individuals, and to acknowledge that they may have had previous negative math experiences, ask questions they can respond to in a math autobiography, a class discussion, or a private conversation. I use math autobiographies to give students an opportunity to tell me what previous teachers did that they found either helpful or unhelpful. Their answers sometimes point out things I do that students find disturbing, such as, "My teacher let the class get pretty noisy and then she'd just speak louder than the noise." Other responses are windows into the causes of specific problems, such as low participation. Another student wrote, "When I'd ask my teacher for help with a problem, she'd say, 'What's not to get?' so I stopped asking questions."

Find ways to encourage memories of positive school experiences, and use those memories to activate students' motivation. It is likely that all students can recall at least one positive experience related to school, if not to math specifically. Trigger these positive memories by asking questions such as the following:

- Can you remember a time when you were excited about something at school? You may have been nervous, but when you started kindergarten did you feel you were now a "big kid" too? Did you look forward to experiencing some of the good things you had heard about, like making handprints, playing on cool playground equipment, getting new school supplies, learning new things, and seeing your friends every day?
- Can you recall a time when you were proud to answer a question or when you got a good grade after studying hard?
- Did you ever help a friend understand something in class or invite a classmate to join your group when he or she didn't have a partner?

After you discuss some of these positive experiences with your students, talk about how and why their attitudes toward math changed for the worse at some point before they started your class. Through this process, students begin to build a supportive class community when they hear similarities between their classmates' experiences and their own feelings. Possible questions to prompt this discussion include the following:

- When did you first wake up and not want to go to school or hope it was a weekend?
- What did teachers do that turned you off to school? To math?
- Did you ever lose interest because you weren't learning new things or because you didn't understand things that you thought everyone else *did* understand?

You may need to stimulate these discussions about negativity with your own experiences; this sharing will also increase the bonds between you and your students. Think about times when you felt overly challenged, out of place, or ready to give up. How did that feel? In all likelihood, these feelings were similar to many of the emotions your students deal with. Share those experiences with your students, along with coping mechanisms or solutions that helped you deal with and overcome your negativity.

♣ STRATEGY: Have Students Assess You

Report cards and grades are often high-stress experiences that remain as strong negative memories. Clearly explain your policies concerning credit for partial work (if a serious attempt was made to solve the problem) and for homework corrections. Point out that simply copying the question will help students build their math brains, and after they review their homework, they will have more success when they return to problems they copied down instead of facing a blank page.

I offer students the opportunity to decide on categories in which they will assess me and then give me report card grades. My recent 7th grade class selected the following areas: *kindness, organization, fairness, friendliness, favoritism, knows material, funny, listens,* and *explains material well.*

In their first grading period, the grades were highest in these categories: *kindness, friendliness, fairness, favoritism* (indicating a lack thereof), and *knows material.* However, many of my students felt that I needed to improve my listening and explaining skills. I was disappointed, because I thought I'd been doing well in those areas. I asked for some specific examples (they could offer them anonymously in writing or orally) and received valid feedback. I had a colleague observe my classes a few times and focus on those two areas. She helped me identify times when I could have done a better job of listening and explaining, and I implemented changes. The experience was valuable, and I continue to show students that I value their opinions each time I have them write my report cards. My hope is that I model appropriate responses to their feedback as I continue to be a learner.

———————————

When you help your students build a positive attitude toward math, they become engaged in the material and motivated to excel in mathematics because they value it. When you offer experiences and opportunities that inspire your students to measure, question, and analyze things around them, they will want to acquire the knowledge and mathematical tools necessary to achieve those goals. Once you reopen doors that were previously closed by negative feelings, math is revealed to students as an accessible, valuable tool to help them understand, describe, and have more control over the world in which they live.

2

Understanding and Planning Achievable Challenge

> The secret of getting started is breaking your complex overwhelming tasks into small manageable tasks, and then starting on the first one.
> —Mark Twain

Imagine the following scenarios and the personal reactions that would likely arise from them.

- You are dropped off at the top of a ski resort's steepest run when you've only had experience on the beginner slopes.
- You have to spend your day on the bunny hill when you're an expert skier.
- You play a game of darts with the target two feet away.
- You play a game of darts with the target 200 feet away.
- You are a 3rd grade student trying to do a crossword puzzle designed for experts.
- You are an adult trying to do a crossword puzzle designed for children.

In each of these extremes, you would feel either frustrated or bored, depending on your level of *achievable challenge*. Reflecting on those personal feelings helps us understand what it feels like for students who do not have the foundational background to understand the new topics the class is learning or who have already mastered the current material and are bored by having to listen to lessons that don't introduce new information for them.

Math classes often move through the curriculum in lockstep, regardless of students' individual levels of mastery of previous or prerequisite concepts.

Even students who do not have negative attitudes about math in general will likely become bored when lessons repeat what they have already mastered. Similarly, students who don't have the necessary background skills or who can't follow the lesson instruction will become frustrated.

Incorporating Challenge into the Equation

For students to be engaged in their learning, they need relevant, achievable challenge. Achievable-challenge tasks require students to exert mental effort, performing a task that is just difficult enough to hold their interest but not so difficult that they give up in frustration. When this balance is struck, it actually becomes pleasurable to focus the mind for long periods of time.

You know it would do nothing to improve your students' math negativity to give them a test on a topic they mastered years before, such as testing 5th grade students on adding single-digit positive integers. They may all ace the test, but unless students feel that the achievement is a challenge, they feel no intrinsic satisfaction from their success.

Challenge is a powerful motivator when students take on a task they find meaningful and, through their efforts and perseverance, succeed. Because (as described in Chapter 1) the amygdala's filter can block learning when students feel stressed, frustrated, or overwhelmed, the ideal learning situation is one of individualized, *achievable* challenge. Achievable challenge is powerful because each experience with success leads to increased levels in the brain of a neurotransmitter called dopamine, which is accompanied by a sense of pleasure and decreased anxiety in response to various stressors, including math (Kienast et al., 2008). The intrinsic rewards of solving a challenging problem are powerful, and the dopamine-pleasure reaction encourages subsequent similar pursuits.

From authentic achievements with suitable challenges, students experience the reward of their competence, effort, and perseverance. Once this happens, math negativity declines and resilience builds. Students see themselves as learners and inventors of math as they develop confidence, curiosity, flexibility, perseverance, interest, and inventiveness. For students with considerable negative baggage, teachers should use differentiated approaches to provide opportunities for success where there is challenge, but with enough support

GRAY MATTER ⚙️

The Dopamine-Reward Cycle

Dopamine is a learning-friendly neurotransmitter associated with pleasurable feelings, motivation, memory, and focus. Its release and suppression are controlled by a deep brain structure called the nucleus accumbens (NAc). Humans instinctively put a positive value on actions or thoughts that have been associated with past dopamine release and pleasure.

One stimulus for dopamine release is the awareness of making a correct choice. The brain values the correct response more when the question or problem solved is in the person's challenge range, rather than requiring only minimum risk or effort. The rise and fall of dopamine levels in response to the satisfaction of a correct choice (answer) is a way of learning information gained by participation—answering a question. The brain favors and repeats actions that release more dopamine. In this way, dopamine helps us decide among alternatives.

Dopamine release not only causes a pleasurable feeling, but it also decreases anxiety and increases memory. One study among rats has shown that the release of dopamine in the hippocampus activates the synapses among nerve cells, creating stronger connections and leading to long-term memory storage (Li, Cullen, Anwyl, & Rowan, 2003). Thus, if we make correct decisions, the dopamine reward of pleasure strengthens that memory. When dopamine levels in the amygdala are higher, there is more communication from the amygdala to the anterior cingulated cortex, a part of the prefrontal cortex associated with problem solving. This effect is associated with study subjects who scored lower on tests of anxiety. The research team surmised that greater levels of dopamine release decrease one's tendency to experience events as stressful (Kienast et al., 2008).

As students continue to progress academically, the dopamine reward cycle continues to generate pleasurable feelings. These pleasurable feelings in turn motivate perseverance and increase tolerance for mistakes.

that failure is rare. (You'll find descriptions of many such approaches in the following chapters.)

Learning from Video Games

Video games are an example of the lure of achievable challenge because they help students reach personally desirable goals. The goals are not tangible prizes, money, or public acknowledgment, but they are usually associated with the goals of the game—mastering the skills to save the day, reach the treasure, solve the puzzles, or conquer the opponent. These goals can be translated into mathematics as long as we use the model of achievable challenge (through differentiation and individualization) and connect our teaching goals with students' personal goals and interests. Translating the video game model of incremental challenge to the classroom, at the appropriate level for students' abilities, results in lessons that are satisfying, motivating, and strategically designed to build mastery.

In a study of what makes video games so captivating, the key element was found to be variable *ability-based challenge* for players. The most popular games took players through increasingly challenging levels as they became more and more skillful. As skill improved, the next challenge motivated new mastery to just the right extent such that the player could reach the next goal with practice and persistence. The most motivating video games are ones in which players make the correct move about 80 percent of the time at first, then build up to the 100 percent or so required to reach the next level. In these games, players feel challenged enough and intrinsically rewarded enough to continue the exercise (Malone, 1982).

The challenge of promoting students' unconscious selection of input (that is relevant to a classroom environment) is now greater than ever, because there is more competition from the multisensory stimuli that pervade their wider environments. Computer games, iPods, and cell phones are not going away. Even when students are temporarily "unplugged," their brains may continue processing the large amount of data accumulated during their time spent engaged with these technologies.

Interestingly, some computer games may actually increase sustained focus, creative problem solving, and perseverance through challenge as players' optimism and expertise develop simultaneously. Moreover, some games teach skills that may not be embedded in the standardized school curriculum, such as teamwork, data analysis, decision making, and digital literacy (Gee, 2003).

We cannot go back to a time before the "bells and whistles" of modern technology, but we can use what we have learned about the positive response and sense of fulfillment associated with computer games that offer achievable challenge. We can develop academic lessons using the principles that make these technologies so compelling. You can use strategies to provide experiences and develop student goals based on *individualized realistic challenges*. These challenges are motivating because of student interest, they are supported by desired goals and positive intrinsic reinforcement, and they are geared to students' individual learning strengths and mastery levels. At the same time, these challenges take into consideration—and seek to avoid—the negative effects of frustration and boredom, those emotional stressors that block information flow to the prefrontal cortex and reduce students to their reactive state of fight/flight/freeze neural processing. This effect is especially problematic in math because so much of the material requires background knowledge, which in turn requires fully open connections between the PFC and the memory storage networks. Our challenge is to help our students' brains work at this low-stress, high-engagement level by providing lessons and homework that maximize interest and attention and reverse math negativity.

Contributing to the Effort

Guiding students' progress through the math curriculum in a way that promotes successful, long-term learning and positive math attitudes requires paying attention to their different levels of achievable challenge and different learning strengths. Through this construct, students become engaged and open to acquiring the skills they need to progress to the next level. Individualized achievable challenge connects students to knowledge by communicating high expectations, confirming that they have the capacity to reach these goals, and showing them how to access the tools and support they need to reach goals they consider desirable. Using achievable challenge, the bar does not need to be lowered—access is available at the appropriate level, and students are supported using knowledge of their individual strengths and background knowledge. By engaging students and ensuring that they succeed frequently, we empower those who have math negativity by providing a sense of their growing knowledge of and appreciation for math (Dweck, 2000).

Individualized plans that set students on appropriately challenging, goal-directed paths, and that have the benefit of maximum brain engagement, are time consuming. Your support is needed to help students make connections to prior knowledge, to collaborate on and determine mutually acceptable goals, and to provide direct instruction when needed. Instructional strategies include conferencing, encouraging student self-assessment and reflection, and providing specific, timely feedback so students can make corrections in the context of an authentic application. (These supports are all discussed in terms of specific strategies in the following chapters.)

The costs of extra planning time are offset, however, by significant rewards, as evidenced by students' successes and their improved confidence and attitudes, as well as their achievement on standardized tests. Another likely benefit you may enjoy is a reduction in the time required for basic behavioral management in the classroom.

Celebrating Achieved Challenges

While teachers may not have the benefit of computerized special effects to acknowledge a student's newly achieved challenge, recognition is valuable to reinforce the associated dopamine-pleasure response. We want to sustain students' pleasurable memories of achievement so the dopamine-reward system will fire up in *anticipation* of the next achievable challenge. Memories of successes are particularly valuable when students slip and revert to their previous math negativity.

Csikszentmihalyi (1991) writes about the pleasurable state of "flow" that accompanies problem solving when the problem is neither too easy nor too challenging. If the planning has gone well, that state of flow (or dopamine pleasure) will be a motivating, self-sustaining reward.

Other ways to celebrate and maintain positive memories and knowledge include the following:

• Have students teach the new skill to someone else.
• Have students keep a list of achievements in their math journals or write them on a wall chart.

- Take a photo of the final achievement (even if it is something as simple as a well-solved math problem).
- Have students compose a note to their parents, and add your own comments.
- Provide opportunities for students to transfer the new skills to new situations—an approach I call "celebrate and cement." Consider how the achieved challenge can be the basis for an independent project.
- Incorporate a record of progress as part of your students' ongoing assessment if the achievement is part of a progressive plan.

Balancing and Building

Achievable challenge can be thought of in terms of two metaphors: balancing a scale and building a structure. As on a scale, achievable challenge reduces negativity by adding positive emotional connections to math through skill-building and confidence-building exercises. Additionally, when a building is constructed, the foundation needs to be the strongest part. Likewise, math students' learning strengths and background skills form the educational foundation upon which the framework—the achievable challenges that propel students along their academic path—is built. Using achievable challenge to build student confidence and develop student success is the positive reinforcement that balances—and ultimately reverses—negative emotions toward math. Your students will acquire a new outlook on math and go from feeling like captives of math class to captains of their own math minds. The fight/flight/freeze response will no longer be their default, involuntary reaction to mathematics. With prefrontal cortexes engaged, amygdalas wide open, and dopamine pumps full, they will be ready to go forward and boldly take on challenges.

Planning for Achievable Challenge

Differentiating allows you to plan the best links between your students' learning strengths, background knowledge and mastery, and level of achievable challenge. In the not-too-distant future, neuroimaging and aligned cognitive testing will help us match individual differences to the appropriate level of challenge and the best strategies for our students. Advances in computer instruction will increase opportunities for individualized learning using digital, video, and audio media, and even virtual-reality avatars.

For now, though, your students need *you* to mine your knowledge of their learning differences, interests, skills, and strengths to adapt learning groups, classroom instruction, homework, multimedia support, motivational influences, out-of-class tutoring, and instructional strategies and allow each student to work at his or her maximum level of achievable challenge.

Learning Strengths: Map Readers and Explorers

For the purposes of math class instruction, most students can be differentiated into two general categories of learning strengths: Map Readers or Explorers. These names don't stigmatize students, evoke parental distress that children are being sorted into a category that is mistakenly considered less academic, or limit the strategies worth trying. I determine placement between these categories not by formal testing but by evidence accumulated in various ways.

I recognize Map Readers because they often like to work independently, but they are most comfortable when they have specific instructions or procedures to follow. They often take more time and work deliberately, showing all their steps on homework or taking detailed notes in class or during group work. Explorers are the students who want to skip the detailed instructions and jump right into figuring things out by trial and error. These students are not likely to use estimation, even when required on homework, because they want to get right to the solving of the problem. When they make errors on tests, these students are often able to solve the problem correctly when I require them to talk me through the sequence of their calculations or write out all the steps. They also tend to understand and give good examples of concepts, but they need to be reminded that showing their work lets their brain focus on one thing at a time and reduces the errors they make.

Map Readers share some characteristics of the linguistic and logical-mathematical intelligence groupings originally proposed by Gardner (1983) and the learning styles of auditory, sequential, and analytic learners. Among their distinct characteristics and preferences, Map Readers

- Prefer problems with definite answers and procedures to follow.
- Prefer new skills to be teacher-modeled.
- Process information in a "parts-to-whole" dynamic, with learning activities broken down into sequential steps.
- Are comfortable with logical, orderly, and structured approaches.
- Are adept at using words to understand and convey information, but may prefer written to oral responses.
- Want time to practice before sharing their ideas or answers.
- Appreciate early, frequent feedback or coaching sessions.
- Respond to cause-and-effect relationships, codes, sequences, and guided pattern recognition with early explanations showing all the steps required to develop a procedural understanding.
- Enjoy working independently and typically do not respond well to mixed-ability groupings.
- Enjoy journaling or responsive note taking/note making.

Note taking and note making allow students to personally relate to the information they write in their notes. A page is folded vertically, and on the left students write formal notes. On the right, they respond to any personal feelings they have when they think about the information they write. For example, "It makes sense that division is like a row of subtractions, because multiplication is like a row of additions" or "I wonder if a fraction is the same thing as a division problem because when I divide the top number by the denominator I get a decimal that seems the same as the fraction." Questions or concerns can also be included in the note-making column, such as, "I don't really know why this works. I get the right answer, but I'm still confused" or "Why do some problems ask me to round off to hundredths and others to the nearest tenth? It bugs me that they seem so random."

Explorers, on the other hand, share some characteristics of the spatial and bodily-kinesthetic groups and the learning styles of global, big-picture, exploratory learners (Gardner, 1983). Among their distinct characteristics and preferences, Explorers

- Want to use their imagination—they try things before reading or hearing the detailed instructions.
- Prefer discovery and exploratory learning in which they are free to experiment, create, construct, and explore topics of study independently before direct instruction or modeling.
- Process information best when the topic is introduced as a "big picture" and then broken down into parts.
- Use visualization memory strategies.
- Enjoy more choice and opportunities for innovation.
- Find it helpful to draw diagrams, use graphic organizers, or make models and then add their own elaborations in response to new mathematical information.
- Recognize a pattern and then find thematic and cross-curricular links beyond mathematics.
- Relate to inquiry projects that are more open-ended.
- Move their bodies to connect with information, solve problems, and convey ideas.
- Work well with others in various groupings.
- Are drawn into topics by people who use math in their careers or hobbies.
- Respond well to models or manipulatives that help them see where instruction is heading.
- Construct mental patterns to connect prior learning with new knowledge.

Using Students' Learning Strengths

Increasing homogenization of curriculum has effectively limited students' opportunities to discover, strengthen, and take advantage of their talents and interests that lie uncovered in areas outside of the narrow range of subjects that are tested on standardized tests and exit exams. When class time is primarily mandated for the core subjects that will be tested, opportunities to discover intelligences and learning strengths through sports, drama, music, or art are limited.

To address this, you can introduce new units by offering each category of learner—Map Readers and Explorers—at least one specific, targeted activity. Observe what elicits students' interest and successful participation. Interviews and written inventories can provide you with information about activities they like best, their interests, and their hopes for the future.

Once you discover students' learning strengths, consider ways you can apply this knowledge, such as telling students about their strengths, keeping strategy lists, creating flexible groupings and collaborative groups based on strengths or interests, and planning suitable achievable-challenge lessons and homework.

After gathering data about your students, consider meeting with other teachers in interdisciplinary teams to compare notes about successful strategies and students' classroom performance, strengths, and challenges. In elementary school, for example, such meetings can include resource specialists, subject-area teachers, librarians, club supervisors, and athletic coaches. When students have more than one teacher, it helps if teachers coordinate among themselves dates of tests or when papers are due so students are not overly stressed and can get enough sleep.

✤ STRATEGY: Use Multisensory Input

Many teachers spend much of math class lecturing and writing on the board at the front of the room. However, you can reach a greater variety of students' learning strengths when you vary sensory input. Consider playing music at some time during the day as a way to provide novelty, to set the stage for a lesson, to introduce a new concept, or to emphasize a concept while providing another sensory memory for the neuronal circuit. Consider drawing diagrams, graphs, and sketches. Pictures or video clips illustrate how a procedure is used in a job, sport, or hobby and adds "here-me-now" meaning for your students.

"Here-me-now" refers to the way the brain is attracted to things that are personally valued and that have the potential to bring pleasure of satisfaction sooner, rather than later. We want students to develop the capacity to delay immediate gratification, but first they need to be engaged in the process of extending their knowledge. This is not an inherently pleasurable goal for the brain, which is programmed to survive danger and explore novelty for potential pleasure. When we ask students to take on the brain stress of extending their knowledge beyond what they already understand, we are asking them to leave their comfort zones. The lower brain, which determines what sensory input gets access to the higher brain, will attend to new input if there is a previous association with pleasure and a perception that satisfaction or a desired outcome will be directly associated with a new challenge. Starting a new topic by presenting ways that students will soon be able to use the knowledge for something they like, such as building something, working outside on a math investigation, or using the information to relate to sports statistics, gives the lower, pleasure-seeking brain motivation to attend to the lesson.

You can address other learning strengths and provide more multi-sensory input by using hands-on experiences with manipulatives, moving students around the classroom to demonstrate concepts (e.g., constructing "living equations," creating different powers-of-ten numbers with "0" and "1" number cards), or having students represent new information through examples created by small groups and shared with the class using overhead transparencies or an interactive whiteboard screen.

For younger students with shorter attention spans, you can vary the presentation of information within the same period by stimulating several senses. For example, speak in a rhythmic cadence, rhyme, or rap some key phrases (e.g., "You have some apples, you have some oranges, but you can't sum them together 'cause they're still different fruits"). These lessons can also incorporate pictures, realia (a good approach for ELL students), or hand gestures that students mimic for appropriate mathematical procedures (i.e., $+, -, \times, \div, =$).

❖ STRATEGY: Use Flexible Grouping

As noted in *The Final Report of the National Mathematics Advisory Council* (U.S. Dept. of Education, 2008), a national survey asked more than 700 Algebra 1 teachers about the challenges they face. The most frequent written-in response (as opposed to responses chosen from among various options) mentioned "handling different skill levels in a single classroom"

(p. 9). A majority of teachers considered mixed-ability groupings to be a "moderate" or "serious" problem.

The panel's conclusion was that flexible ability grouping, with students at similar levels of achievement, serves students without the flaws of tracking. Because of different math backgrounds, learning strengths, reading skills, and English language proficiency, students have varying levels of achievable challenge in different math topics, further supporting the benefit of flexible groupings.

Flexible groups should be designed so students can move easily between them, depending on their mastery of specific math topics. Within their groups, students can share similar manipulatives and participate in appropriately challenging inquiries and discussions. Your classroom observations will also help correctly place students in appropriate classes and groups for the following year. Obviously, this is particularly useful for students' future teachers who are inclined to differentiate, use approaches best suited to specific students, and accommodate for special needs and strengths.

✤ STRATEGY: Scaffold for Achievable Challenge

Scaffolded instruction facilitates learning at students' achievable-challenge levels by providing a sequence of prompts or intermediate supports in content, materials, or teacher guidance. For example, students who haven't yet mastered "automatic" math facts of single-digit subtraction—necessary to practice the concept of "regrouping" or "borrowing" for subtraction—can learn the new concept more successfully with a set of problems geared toward their achievable-challenge level. Their scaffolded task might be to just *identify* the problems where regrouping is needed, such as 24–19. They can also write answers or estimates for the problems they want to try while avoiding the brain's learning blockade that results from stress associated with work that exceeds their current skill level. Reassure these students that answers are not required now, and they will be able to complete the work after they have more foundational subtraction practice. Explain, though, that you are confident they can *learn* the new regrouping procedure along with their classmates now, and that this is the object of the current lesson. This approach will lower students' stress, thereby allowing them to focus on understanding the concept and preventing them from falling further behind.

Another example of lowering the barrier, not the bar, is to scaffold student practice with calculating an average/mean. Some students can work with whole numbers while others work with decimals and fractions, depending on their specific background knowledge. All students will learn the process of finding the mean, so when the students working with whole numbers build their foundational knowledge, they will be able to apply it to fractions and decimals.

✤ STRATEGY: Support ELLs and Students with Reading Difficulties

English language learners (ELLs) and students with reading disabilities may have trouble keeping up with the class, despite appropriate background knowledge and conceptual development, because they have difficulty comprehending word problems. In these cases, students need reading, language, or memorization strategies to give them access to the relevant material. This targeted support and instruction in specific strategies will help students improve their areas of deficiency, and accommodations—such as having word problems read aloud to them—will also allow students to advance their math abilities. There are several relatively simple strategies that you can use to immediately address these students' needs. For example, math vocabulary words can be matched with pictures from the Internet or prearranged manipulatives used during instruction and kept available for students to use during problem solving. If you make a few of these math vocabulary supports each year, you'll gradually accumulate more and more. Collaboration with other teachers will build this "library" of resources even more efficiently.

The Internet is also a powerful tool that can be used to create and use differentiated strategies. There are numerous Web sites (see Appendix A) that provide different levels of achievable challenge. For example, ELL students will benefit from the inclusion of English (or native-language) captions on an animated math procedure, Explorers will respond to the visuals and add the appropriate skill to their memory circuit, and Map

Readers will see the procedure in a sequential fashion that resonates with their learning strengths. Other Web sites include projects that are differentiated by background knowledge and interest so students can work at their achievable-challenge levels to gain a deeper knowledge about specific topics.

Students with visual-processing difficulties can benefit from the variations in text size, color, and font that are available with online versions of textbooks and worksheets. In addition, many computers can be programmed to translate text into spoken English or a foreign language—a novel accommodation that will resonate with many students. Producing calculations and answers in computer-based templates supports students who have difficulty keeping numbers in proper columns or rows, and it also allows you to see all their work so you can identify where they might need further instruction. Technological advances can help you be more of a facilitator than a translator or dispenser of knowledge, and they increase your ability to individualize math with students' interests and learning strengths in mind.

♣ STRATEGY: Avoid Student Boredom

To avoid the stress of boredom, which blocks the input of information to the prefrontal cortex and can result in the fight/flight/freeze behaviors of the reactive brain, limit excessive repetition once mastery is evident for individual students. If students complete class work quickly, easily, and correctly, be prepared with more appropriately challenging or higher-level conceptual problems for them. This will allow them to work at their achievable-challenge levels while still engaged in the same topic that their classmates are practicing.

Similarly, too much repetition of previously mastered procedures in homework assignments is a mental turnoff and stressor. You may think students don't know the skill or are lazy when they don't complete homework or show all their steps, especially if it is early in the year and you aren't familiar with their mastery of each topic. To avoid this negativity, have students write down the amount of time they spend on each homework assignment. Use that information, along with their accuracy, to individualize homework into several levels of challenge. Encourage students who have higher skill levels to build their brains' math muscles by trying new approaches to problems beyond the first one that comes to mind, or substitute problems designated in the math book as "challenge" problems for some of their assigned homework. Most math textbooks include the answers to even or odd problems in the back of the book, and some have Web sites that show worked-out homework problems. Look to see which challenge problems have answers, and let students try these and check the answer key to evaluate their work.

♣ STRATEGY: Challenge Gifted Math Students

Gifted math students may grow frustrated in their inability to write as quickly as they mentally calculate. They may also know concepts so well that they devise and automatically apply appropriate procedures without being able to explain what they did procedurally. If your advanced students are resistant—or truly turned off—and lose enthusiasm for math when they are required to show the intermediate steps that never even became conscious in their working memories, try giving them more challenging problems. With these problems, they'll need to show their work for their own sake in order to get the right answer because the numbers are too large for mental math and the procedures are too extensive to be carried out automatically. As part of the process, they will build written math communication skills and you will see where they have incorrect concepts or gaps. In addition, they will come to understand the value of showing their work, not because it is a requirement but because it is helpful.

If the most difficult problems in your math text are still below the level of achievable challenge for some students, consult the math book for the coming year. Because most topics are repeated with the addition of higher conceptual or procedural learning, these texts are likely to have appropriate questions, along with answers for you to use to check student work. This saves you from having to create and solve new problems for each topic. Other sources of appropriate challenge problems for these students are Web sites such as Math Olympiads for Elementary and Middle School (www.moems.org). Highly advanced learners can tackle the Olympiads problems as early as 3rd or 4th grade.

===

Find your own level of achievable challenge by considering what is achievable for *you* in terms of differentiating your students' learning. Consider starting with one or two students or a single unit that allows all learners to become engaged through their different learning strengths. Celebrate your own success by taking time to see the difference you made for your students' achievement, behavior, and attitudes, and be mindful of how you feel when things work. You'll stimulate and strengthen your own neuronal network for differentiating and planning for achievable challenge, and these approaches will become more and more automatic.

3

Examples of Differentiated Planning for Achievable Challenge

....

> Knowing a great deal is not the same as being smart; intelligence is not information alone but also judgment, the manner in which information is collected and used.
>
> —Carl Sagan

To further illustrate how to plan activities and lessons that address students' varying levels of achievable challenge, this chapter examines some specific approaches. In the following examples, notice how students are all learning the same concepts at different levels of challenge in order to maximize success and minimize feelings of frustration and inadequacy.

Working with Shapes

An activity called "Draw My Picture" is especially enjoyable for Map Readers, but it also shows Explorers and students with high mastery of shape information the importance of communication. This activity involves the following steps:

1. Pair students with similar abilities regarding shape recognition and naming (or pair a student with high shape mastery and low communication skills with a student who has high communication skills and low shape mastery).

2. Give each pairing a set of variously shaped manipulatives (realia, drawings, or paper cutouts).

3. Have the partners sit opposite each other with a divider preventing them from seeing the other's work surface.

4. One partner gives verbal instructions for drawing a selected shape. For example, one student might instruct his or her partner to draw a "long triangle with the pointy side down" and then draw a "semicircle, flat side down over the flat top of the triangle" (an ice cream cone).

5. For older children, the verbal instructions could include descriptive vocabulary words they are using in class, such as *right angle, isosceles triangle, diagonal,* or *proportional sides.*

The success of the speaker's verbal communication and the artist's careful following of instructions become immediate feedback when both students see the final drawing. The describer takes satisfaction in accurate communication, and the drawer is proud of his or her attention to the details of the description. They then discuss what was most helpful and what was confusing in the verbal instructions before switching tasks.

Estimating Volume

In this activity, students estimate volumes at different degrees of achievable challenge in homogeneous groupings. The goal is to build their estimation/prediction skills, ability to adapt to new evidence, math communication skills, number-sense skills, and conceptual awareness.

Group 1—Low Complexity. Have students form groups, and give each group a large pitcher of colored water. Explain that each member of the group will fill an 8-ounce cup from the pitcher and predict how high the level will reach when the water is poured into clear bottles of different diameters (e.g., empty soda or juice bottles or measuring cups of different sizes). When they come to a group consensus, students use a marker to indicate their predictions and then pour the colored water into the container and discuss the results. (For assessment purposes, individuals in each group can use differently colored markers to indicate their separate predictions.)

Possible discussion questions and extensions for this activity include the following:

- Why was the level lower/higher than your prediction?
- What do you predict the level will be when you add a second cup of water? (*Students should then make a prediction, add the water, and discuss the results.*)
- How many cups do you predict will be needed to fill up each of the containers? (*Students should then make a prediction, add the water, and discuss the results.*)
- Have students present their findings in the form of a diagram, chart, overhead transparency sketch, graph, other graphic organizer, or group discussion.

Group 2—Medium Complexity (Early Conceptual Thinking). The students in this group do a similar activity but should design the experiment themselves. The goal is still for students to make predictions, but students in this group are only provided with the materials (a pitcher of colored water, clear bottles of various diameters, and an 8-ounce cup), not the step-by-step procedure. Students make predictions and then discuss how they can gather evidence to estimate how many cups of water are needed to fill each container. Have them keep group (or personal) records of their predictions, results, and explanations. Students should be challenged to respond to questions, explain their reasoning for changing predictions, and even come up with any "rules" (i.e., big ideas, concepts) they think apply to the activity. Examples of such rules might include "the wider the diameter, the lower the water level" or, more specifically, "if the diameter of the container is twice that of the previous container, the water level will be exactly one-quarter as high." Encourage more advanced group members to identify two or more ways to complete the experiment and solve the problem.

As you observe your students pouring water from the pitcher into the cup and from the cup into the bottles, invite them to stop after each step and write down any new estimates, based on the evidence they acquire along the way. If they revise their predictions, students should include an explanation about why they did so. Have them keep notes or diagrams about the results of the experiment (encourage them to use terms such as *half, quarter,* or *percent*).

Group 3—High Complexity (More Abstract Conceptual Thinking). Students in this group incorporate metric conversions and look at the ounce markings on a measuring cup. After performing the experiment they design, they pour water from the 8-ounce cup into a measuring cup with metric markings. In addition to the procedure used by Group 2, they also analyze, predict, test, adjust, and develop correlations about the relationship of cups, liters, ounces, and milliliters. They can then discuss ways to find a conversion factor for each of these comparisons (e.g., how many cups are in a liter) and see how that conversion factor also applies to milliliters and ounces.

After all three groups have completed their experiments, they share their experiences and results with the class, emphasizing how they altered predictions based on new evidence. Group 1 students should report first, as this might be their only reportable information, and each subsequent group adds new information to the discoveries of the previous group. Record the class information on a chart or other graphic organizer. The class can then make further predictions from the gathered data, test their conversion factors, and confirm these factors with formal conversion charts.

Ultimately, all students can participate by considering how the information can be transferred—used for purposes other than just the class experiment— such as how different bottle designs create the illusion of a larger volume or the factors to consider when determining cost and the ecologic impact of selling items in large-volume containers. Taking into consideration their different levels of achievable challenge, students can be given differentiated homework assignments. For example, lower-level students can look around the supermarket or in newspaper ads to evaluate how different companies persuade people to buy their products based on the size or design of a container, while higher-level students can determine which is a better value in terms of cost and quantity: a six-pack of 12-ounce soda cans or a liter bottle at the same price. An even better approach is to have students design their own questions that they want to evaluate—an approach that assigns ownership and meaning to their work.

Exploring Number Lines

Number lines are helpful constructions for both Explorers and Map Readers. Explorers can move about the line, and Map Readers can examine and evaluate the designations and patterns in the line. This strategy also allows your students to gain some experience using KWL charts. The KWL strategy activates students' prior knowledge by asking them to identify what they already *know* about a particular topic and write their responses on a chart. Students then set goals specifying what they *want* to learn. At the culmination of the unit, students discuss what they have *learned* and complete the chart, correcting any errors in the K column. Additionally, if students create individual KWL charts, they can build their own goals—things they particularly want to know that are relevant to the coming unit of study.

As a preliminary activity for the number line strategy, the whole class (or the class divided into small groups) is free to explore number lines without a specific assignment. Begin by creating several number lines on large sheets of paper to roll out on the floor, or use masking tape for more permanent lines. After exploring the lines, students meet in mixed groups to create their K and W ideas for a KWL chart. Students then share their ideas for a master chart that you create. As you walk around and listen to students contribute ideas to their first group meeting, you will gain insights about background knowledge that may be different from your own predictions for each student's mastery of the topic. This additional source of differentiation information can be more formalized if each student is assigned a colored pencil with which he or she can add to the group KWL chart.

During subsequent lessons, students can be moved to groups of higher or lower achievable-challenge levels as you observe their participation and understanding within the original heterogeneous groups. Groups well matched to their achievable-challenge levels are guided to progress further along the continuum of activities; students with higher mastery/background levels will eventually reach a conceptual analysis of what the number line means regarding integers. Groups still working at the more basic levels of exploration should be engaged at their appropriate levels of achievable challenge, but they will also benefit from what is going on around them. As they observe other groups engaged in apparently enjoyable activities, they are motivated to continue their explorations and discussions to achieve higher levels and engage in these same activities.

The following activity outlines the differentiation that is possible within homogeneous groupings that capitalize on various levels of achievable challenge.

Group 1—Low Complexity. Do a "modeling demonstration" in which you count aloud as you step forward along the number line from 0 to 5, looking down and counting the numbers as you walk. Students then take turns counting the steps aloud as they walk, stopping whenever they choose and announcing the number of units they walked. The rest of the group confirms this number by looking at the numeral that the "walker" is standing on. When each student has had an opportunity to participate, encourage the group members to discuss what they noticed. Then have them write or sketch their conclusions individually and on a group chart.

Group 2—Medium Complexity (Early Conceptual Thinking). Those who show mastery early on can be in a flexible group for the next section of the unit and advance to addition and subtraction. The student who walks the number line can stop at any point, and the group can take turns asking him or her to take one more step and announce the new number. He or she might choose to look down at the number or to predict the answer before checking.

Extend the activity by asking group members to predict where the volunteer "walker" would be if he or she took one more step, two more steps, three more steps, and so on. The student should then take the appropriate number of steps so the group can check the prediction. The volunteer can also independently make a prediction before taking the steps and checking his or her own prediction.

When every group member has had an opportunity to be the "walker," the group members can turn their observations into a diagram or chart. Students should then use their own words to describe the action. Some may use words that indicate addition, such as, "She moved up 3 squares from 3 and ended on square 6" or "She went forward (or to the right) 3 more squares from 3 and was on number 6." On the board, keep a list of the relevant mathematical terms that students use in their descriptions.

When students look over the words they used to describe moving ahead, forward, or to the right, they may use the word *added,* but this is not as important as seeing the process and describing the predictable result. Along the way, they will discover the process of addition, and they will eventually use this term after they understand its meaning. In subsequent number line walks, encourage students to use the word *add* and write their results in sentences such as, "I was on number 7, then I added 3 more and was on number 10."

It won't be long before students instinctively start experimenting with movement in the opposite direction, and in doing so they will discover the concept of subtraction along a number line. Many options can follow that will help students transfer this new information by mental manipulation to other representations of addition and subtraction, including organizing collections of objects and writing sentences with appropriate conceptual vocabulary.

They can also continue playing the walk-the-line game; for example, either you or group members can request that the volunteer "walker" start on number 9 and move five spaces to the left. Have students make predictions before the volunteer moves, but if the prediction is off, ask students to make a prediction of where the "walker" will be if he or she only moves one or two steps to the left. Then have students make a new prediction about the original assignment (move five spaces to the left), and have the "walker" take the appropriate number of steps. If the prediction is still incorrect, tell students to confer about how they can rethink the process they observed and make more accurate predictions next time. If necessary, have them go back to the earlier practice of counting while watching the squares. The "walker" starts at number 9 and, without first predicting, counts up to 5 aloud as he or she takes five steps along the number line to the left. Encourage students to report on the process aloud, for example, "I started on number 9, walked back 5, and I'm now on number 4."

Encourage group members to follow your coaching model when their classmates make prediction errors. Such encouragement will help students become more skilled at supportive instruction and avoid being critical or taking over the solution from the "walker." Both the "walker" and the guiding group member will enjoy the satisfaction of supportive collaboration and even the dopamine pleasure that accompanies kindness, optimism, intrinsic satisfaction, generosity, and positive peer interactions. Stress will remain low, and students will return to the number line activities with positive feelings, thanks to the activation of their dopamine-pleasure circuit in anticipation of a positive experience.

I've observed students engaged in this activity on many occasions. They discussed why some of their predictions were correct and some were not.

Their communication was enthusiastic, but rarely pushy. They felt the comfort of sharing ideas and a communal responsibility to communicate patiently so the group would continue to explore and build knowledge together.

The value of not forcing the words *addition* or *subtraction* or the symbols + or − at this time is that the students are able to construct their own concepts, rather than memorize an abstract formula. When the correct words and symbols are added later, they will create an accurate and durable neural pathway, and they will have a tangible meaning because students already created the concept on their own and experienced the intrinsic reward of achieving a challenge they valued.

Group 3—High Complexity (More Abstract Conceptual Thinking). For those students whom you observe developing mastery in the middle level of complexity, such that they are now below their appropriate achievable-challenge level, or for students who have mastery of the foundational material, the activities described here are more appropriately challenging. These students work with peers to brainstorm what other things they might do with a number line, or they follow your guidance to lead them to the concept of multiples and multiplication. For example, you can ask, "Can you find a way to see what happens and how to predict where the 'walker' will be if he walks two squares at a time?"

Eventually, when students have mastered subtraction along the number line, they will want to know how to write or label the negative integers below or to the left of the 0. They will ask you to add more tape or paper to the left of the 0 (or you could preemptively add it before the next math session) to explore negative integers. Discussing, predicting, and asking you for direct instruction (now they *want* to know what you *have* to teach them), they are now in an ideal situation for motivated learning and perseverance through mistakes or obstacles. First, encourage them to confirm their understanding using prediction. Ask, "Where will the 'walker' be if she starts at 7 and takes 7 steps, 9 steps, or 11 steps to the left?" Students should take turns standing on a number and predicting, along with the group, where they will be if they take various numbers of steps to the left before they actually move.

At this stage, continued use of prediction and checking for understanding builds mathematical reasoning and is a more comfortable (i.e., lower-risk) and enjoyable (because it involves movement, dopamine, and peers) way to practice than with paper-and-pencil drills. This approach is also more appropriate, because the task is not to use abstract symbols for *negative* or *subtraction,* but to build the concepts that students will later connect with those symbols. This form of concept construction avoids the inevitable confusion concerning the difference between the symbol – as a negative sign and the same symbol as a sign for subtraction.

Encourage students to find words to describe what these negative numbers represent to them. They may say, "Three down from 1" or "Three on the other side of the 0." As with subtraction, these created words become owned concepts because students develop their own understanding. They now have valuable tools for mentally manipulating and strengthening the developing concept of negative numbers.

Along the way, observe how different students walk the line, and ask them to describe their thinking. You will find evidence identifying Explorers who first take the steps, then develop unifying rules or concepts that build their understanding of negative numbers. You'll also observe Map Readers drawing diagrams or notes, making their own small number lines, or verbalizing the steps sequentially before considering a unifying concept.

After students in Group 3 understand movement along a number line, the next step is to have them manipulate objects to successfully demonstrate that 3 plus 4 adds up to 7, and later that 7 "take away" 3 is 4. As they make these constructions, prompt them to think aloud and describe what they are doing in their own words. Groups should operate with the ground rule that members can disagree, agree, or add to the speaker's explanation only after he or she is finished. Listening to these discussions provides you with powerful formative assessment information as you make checkmarks next to the names of students who are ready to move to a higher level of achievable challenge.

Students will vary in the amount of time they need to predict, correct, practice, and observe before they are very clear on a new process or procedure and are ready to simplify and unify the concept with the new words used in the formal description of negative numbers. When the physical activity makes sense and they can communicate their understanding, they are ready to grasp the higher conceptual and abstract representations of mathematics with numbers, symbols, operational signs, formulas, and equations. Without these intermediate connecting steps, they might get correct answers, but they will be memorized rote answers without the conceptual comprehension that builds the neural networks necessary for math knowledge.

As you would with most group collaborations, call a warning time a few minutes before students are to stop gathering new data, and have them discuss what they noticed. This time allows students who did not get a chance to participate to do so. When time is called again, they should write or sketch their conclusions individually, then on a group chart. Before they present their findings, however, review the group's presentation material to see if it is the right time for the rest of the class to hear the information. It might be beyond the achievable-challenge comprehension level of other students until they progress further in their own investigations.

If this is the case, explain your reason to the group, go over any errors with them, support further investigations they propose if other groups need more time, and challenge them to prepare their presentation to the whole class with clarity for students who are just beginning to understand the concept. One option to build their depth of understanding and build communication skills is for them to prepare presentations of the material in several ways, including different modes of sensory input (e.g., visual, auditory, demonstration of the steps they took) so they connect with the learning strengths of Explorers and Map Readers.

Understanding Division

After your unit opening to assess prior knowledge of the topic and to ignite motivation, model the following activity with manipulatives for the class. The goal is for students to understand the concept of division as a means of breaking larger quantities into specified numbers of portions and to recognize that the process (which, early on, does not need to be called *division*) is a tool for predicting how many objects will be in each new grouping based on the goal (i.e., how many smaller groupings are needed).

Working back from that goal, this activity uses manipulatives as a concrete representation of the division process. One way to assess prior knowledge is to demonstrate a few examples with manipulatives and count the number of objects in each of the smaller groups; after a few demonstrations, ask students to write their predictions for the outcome of the next demonstration on a piece of paper or their personal whiteboards. Feedback from this exercise will help you plan the flexible groups for the following activity.

Group 1—Low Complexity. This group consists of the students whose predictions, after your modeling with manipulatives, were almost all incorrect, even after you gave corrective feedback on the early questions. This group will develop predivision skills by playing games or "sharing" activities. Start by giving the group 10 manipulatives, such as small cubes, and asking them how they would share the cubes among their group of five students (numbers can be adjusted for the size of the group). They can follow their learning strengths and work individually or in pairs at first. Map Readers may want to think first, then discuss their idea, and finally distribute the cubes accordingly. Explorers who like to move or manipulate before sharing their thoughts can do so. When the group meets to discuss, have individual students or pairs of students explain why they did what they did.

Next, using 15 cubes, have each student predict how many cubes each group member will get if the cubes are evenly shared. Students then check their predictions by manipulating the cubes to see if they were correct. Continue this procedure with different numbers of cubes, then with different numbers of group members (pairs or triplets, for example). Students record their data, discuss their findings, and prepare a summary or diagram of their interpretations.

Group 2—Medium Complexity (Early Conceptual Thinking). This group consists of those students who, after some corrective feedback, made correct predictions and could explain their reasoning while you modeled the manipulative division for the whole class. Members of this group can start with their own manipulatives, but they will soon be ready to move on to a greater challenge.

Using real or plastic pennies and groups of five students, ask students how many 10-cent pencils, for example, each of the five group members could "buy" if 100 pennies are distributed equally. Continue with other questions about purchasing things that cost 10 cents, then 20, to determine how many items each group member could "buy." After using their preferred method (e.g., orally, in a graphic organizer) to show their success with the

10- or 20-cent items, students can experiment with the challenge of buying 15-cent items, following the rule that every group member must get exactly the same number of items.

As with all group-learning activities, prepare students by sharing with them the rules of group work, such as the rule that *every* person in the group must be able to explain what the group is doing, and why the group is doing it, or else the entire group's work is not considered successful.

Group 3—High Complexity (More Abstract Conceptual Thinking). This group is likely to have students who already know how to do division with remainders. These students may form a group that breaks off from the medium-complexity group when you see that they need a higher level of achievable challenge, or you may have done a preassessment that revealed background knowledge that logically puts them in this high-complexity group from the beginning.

These students can use real or plastic pennies to answer questions about purchasing items (e.g., small blocks worth one price and large blocks worth a higher price) that cost 10 and 20 cents. They then evaluate the worth of varying numbers of small blocks, then large blocks, then mixed blocks. They eventually move on to distributing the pennies equally, then the blocks representing the value of a specific number of pennies.

Soon, you may find that some group members begin writing calculations with the appropriate mathematical symbols. They are also likely to use the term *remainder* when they use a small block and a large block to represent 30 cents and follow the requirement that every group member gets exactly the same value in blocks.

Numerous options are available for these students. You can ask them to do a fair division of products that cannot be done with the limitations of 10- and 20-cent blocks and incorporate pennies, along with blocks, to create portions of equivalent value. Students can discuss the concept of a *remainder* using their own words and then write a narrative or play script depicting the remainder as an animate object. This can become part of the subsequent class instruction about remainders or fractional answers for division problems. Skits can be videotaped for next year's class.

Another option is to give this group newspaper advertising sections or supermarket flyers with ads offering items at two different prices depending on whether, for example, you purchase one for $.50 or three for $1.00. Have students cut out ads for things they like and explore methods (practical or fanciful) to find out how much the items will individually cost at the new price and how much money they would need to purchase one for each member of the class. Students can then make posters using the original ad and the ideas they had for solving the problems you suggested. These can also become part of the class instructional material when the other students are ready to make these same kinds of calculations. The experience will be motivating for students in this group because it is at their achievable-challenge level, requires them to be creative, has options for different learning strengths, and is valued for its usefulness for future classes.

A Whole-Class Activity for All Groups. Through this activity, students develop their own ideas about remainders and experience the valuable social lesson of fairness. This activity is also an opportunity to demonstrate situations in which multiple opinions can all be correct.

Divide the class into three-person groups, and ask students how they would divide seven large blocks so each group member receives an equal share. Impractical but fanciful solutions, such as pretending to cut remainder blocks into pieces, are great opportunities for fun and creativity. Although the groups are working on background understanding for division with remainders, the concepts they build and then write, draw, or perform become motivating "advertisements" for subsequent lessons about fractions without using the word *fraction*.

The words and representations that students use become memory links—as do the positive feelings and fun (reinforced by dopamine) they have while exploring the block problems with their groups. As a result, the subsequent fraction unit will have an established neural network with which to link new learning, and students will approach fractions with more optimism and resilience.

I have groups keep word lists or make sketches during the inquiry about the extra block so that I can reestablish a link to this block activity in later lessons. Because they can be creative and not necessarily practical during the block exploration, my students' ideas reflect many ideas, including sawing the blocks into pieces, throwing them away, buying extras from other groups, and sharing with another group on a rotating cycle (each would take the extra ones home on alternate days). They draw delightfully creative sketches and write words that I later incorporate onto a class chart, such as *borrow, lend, divide, break up, cut up, equal parts, pieces, whole, half,* and *quarter.* I post this chart, and their sketches, when we begin our fraction unit. Further along in the fraction unit, I return the original charts and sketches to the individual groups. For groups 1 and 2, I write the more "formal" math terms below their original words, and I invite group 3 students to write the terms or symbols they believe are appropriate.

At the end of the day, take time to give your own brain a chance to acknowledge your successes. Did you reduce a student's math negativity or engage even one student through his or her individualized level of achievable challenge? Did you demonstrate something students valued and enjoyed about mathematics? Did a reluctant student feel comfortable participating and risk making a mistake? If so, you moved a student closer to a positive math attitude and much more. If your students experienced the optimism of progress in their range of achievable challenge, that positive experience strengthened one of their neural math networks. The day was a success because this neural pathway became stronger and closer to becoming their default pathway—the one to which their brains will revert when they approach new challenges with resilience. Good for you!

4

Reducing Mistake Anxiety

....

I had problems with [my] math teacher. When I asked a question, she
wouldn't answer and [would] say I should have been listening, even though
I was listening, just her explanation wasn't so great.

—Yasmin, *7th grade student*

With the exception of errors that result from carelessness or incomplete
basic arithmetic facts, the errors that students make in math tend to be
consistent. The most common involve incorrectly applying a procedure or
an algorithm learned by rote memorization. Such errors occur when
students have not developed the mathematical reasoning that accompanies
constructing the mental patterns of concepts; procedures and facts learned
only by rote memory are not available for successful transfer to new
situations.

As in other subjects, students have misconceptions about mathematics.
These misconceptions hinder the learning process because they are strongly
embedded into neural networks that have been activated again and again.
Students need tangible experiences to break these misconceptions.

Eliminating mathematical misconceptions is difficult, and merely repeating a lesson or providing extra time for practice will not help. A better approach
is to show students common errors and help them examine completed sample
problems that demonstrate these common errors. This method also gives you
an opportunity to reinforce critical foundational skills.

Making Common Errors

Multidigit Addition. An example of a common error is $54 + 37 = 811$. This error occurs when students line up the numbers 54 and 37 in columns and write the sums of each column: $4 + 7 = 11$ and $5 + 3 = 8$.

Multidigit Subtraction. A common error occurs when students subtract whichever digit is smaller from the larger digit. For example, $42 - 29 = 27$ because $9 - 2 = 7$ and $4 - 2 = 2$. Later, this error is repeated with negative integers, so that students write $45 - 55 = 10$.

Combining Like Terms. Another concept that needs to be constructed with a framework of experiential learning is that one can add and subtract only *like terms* (i.e., objects of the same category, same units of measurements). Unless this concept is learned with complete understanding in elementary school, it will continue to confuse students when they move on to common denominators and the simplification of algebraic equations. An example of a common error in this category is $2a + 2 = 4a$.

Adding and Subtracting Decimals. Applying the rule they memorized for adding whole numbers, students may line up the numbers on the right side, instead of lining them up based on decimal points. For example, they may write

$$\begin{array}{r} 123.4 \\ -4.593 \\ \hline \end{array}$$

instead of

$$\begin{array}{r} 123.4 \\ -\quad 4.593 \\ \hline \end{array}$$

Zero as a Placeholder. Unless students learn about place value early on, they confuse 0 as a placeholder with a 0 that doesn't change the value of the number. The respective errors would be $3.04 = 3.4$ and $3.40 < 3.400$. This same confusion leads to the mistaken conception that in order to multiply decimals by 10, you just add a 0. Students learn to "add a zero" from working with positive and negative whole numbers, but this solution does not work with decimals and fractions.

Adding and Multiplying Fractions. The most common error students make when they add fractions results from adding the numerators and denominators without first changing the fractions so that they have common denominators. It would not be unusual for a student to see

⅔ + ⅘, then add the numerators $(2 + 4 = 6)$ and denominators $(3 + 5 = 8)$ and conclude that ⅔ + ⅘ = ⅝.

Similarly, students are confused when they are told, without conceptual understanding, why they need to *multiply* numerators and denominators across when multiplying fractions, especially since they are told they cannot *add* numerators and denominators across when adding fractions. The best way to eliminate this misconception is to allow students to work with math manipulatives when they first work with fractions. This approach allows students to visualize denominators and numerators broken down into their basic parts. Further along, confusion about the nature of addition and multiplication will result in the common errors of applying the distributive, associative, and commutative rules to subtraction and division.

"Multiplication Always Results in a Larger Number." This statement is true for positive whole numbers. However, it is not true for fractions and negative numbers. Students latch onto the misconception that this statement is true in all cases because of initial experiences with positive whole numbers. Instead of saying, "one-half *times* eight," try saying, "one-half *of* eight." The use of the word *of* in this problem (i.e., when a fraction and a whole number are multiplied together) informs students that the answer will be less than eight.

Rates and Ratios Written as Whole Numbers or Fractions. Students need to understand that ratios and rates are about relationships between numbers, not the numbers themselves. For example, they may write "2 : 2" or "2 to 2" as 1. If they do, they are missing the concept of rates as a comparison of two different factors (such as miles in relation to hours), so they don't understand why a single number or a mixed number does not represent a comparison and cannot be a rate.

Creating the Right Environment for Younger Students

What we know about the brain suggests that suitable learning environments for young students can differ in some respects from what is suitable for older students. This is due to two important characteristics evident in young children: tolerance for mistakes and innate curiosity.

GRAY MATTER

Trial and Error

Much of what we do or say is based on the brain's interpretation of information stored in memory from prior experiences. Most of our decisions are predictions made on an unconscious level, guided by these memories. Memories of decisions are embedded with the pleasure or displeasure that resulted from previous predictions. As previous experiences build, so does the brain's stored network of data; as a result, our response to new input becomes more accurate.

Through curiosity, trial and error, and the dopamine-mediated pleasure from correct responses and the negative feelings from erroneous responses, our brains are better able to interpret the environment. The brain becomes more and more accurate in anticipating (predicting) what action (answer) is correct (will bring pleasure). These predictions send out signals to the parts of the brain that control our actions, words, or answers to questions. The older children get and the more experiences they have, the more their thinking, reflective prefrontal cortex can modulate the emotional (involuntary, reactive) response of the lower brain. Through trial and error, mistakes, and correct choices, the brain builds neural tracks to preserve and repeat the rewarding behavior. For students and others, this means that after making an incorrect prediction (answer), the next time the question comes up, prediction accuracy is better because the faulty information in the circuit has changed.

Research suggests that young children are usually comfortable making mistakes. In children younger than eight, the areas of the brain involved in cognitive control show strong activation following positive feedback, and stress-reactive regions are *not* activated by negative feedback (Crone, Donohue, Honomichl, Wendelken, & Bunge, 2006; Van Duijvenvoorde, Zanolie, Rombouts, Raijmakers, & Crone, 2008). If you are a teacher of younger students, you are the caretaker of their precious creative potential. Challenge builds skills, and without sufficient challenge, their math brains won't grow.

You want your students to remain comfortable making some mistakes so they will be willing to challenge themselves in the years to come.

Innate curiosity is something we are born with, and young children retain much of this quality. From infancy, young brains need to make sense of their world in order to survive. Innate curiosity is critical to promote this exploration, and it unconsciously drives behavior. Through exploration, children gradually construct neural networks of categories (e.g., patterns, schema), and as exploration and experience continue, the networks expand to accommodate more detail. Networks are modified in response to mistakes (i.e., incorrect predictions based on existing information) as students make more accurate connections between what was predicted and what was

GRAY MATTER

Age-Related Changes

In children up to eight or nine years old, the dopamine-modulating reward center in the nucleus accumbens reacts strongly to positive feedback (activating the prefrontal cortex) and minimally to negative feedback. In older children, increased activation still occurs in the PFC when dopamine is released in response to positive feedback (particularly in response to correct answers/predictions). However, the greatest age-related change is the higher reactivity of the NAc to negative feedback and the accompanying drop in dopamine, decrease in pleasure, and reduced input through the amygdala filter to the PFC. The NAc increases in reactivity through the teen years, then settles down into the adult pattern of less sudden, profound emotional shifts (Crone et al., 2006).

The high response to positive feedback in younger children is neuro-*logical* because their brains need motivation to keep exploring and making sense of the world. In upper elementary school, things begin to change. Because the prefrontal cortex is more reactive to the drop in dopamine release by the NAc that occurs with mistake recognition, students from about 6th grade through high school are affected more by negative feedback and less by positive feedback. Mistakes become high-stress experiences, and the risk of making mistakes, especially in front of classmates, limits their opportunities to learn.

experienced (i.e., sensory input). This process goes on without conscious awareness.

Because young students' brains are driven more by curiosity than by sensitivity to error embarrassment, you can be more direct and call on them to answer questions even if they don't volunteer. This approach is often necessary for younger children, because their brains haven't developed much attention control, and they need you to pull them into the lesson by direct methods, such as saying their names and asking for responses.

Reducing Negative Attitudes Toward Mistakes

The following strategies apply not to errors made on tests, but to mistakes made in front of classmates. We begin with a couple of general strategies to encourage thoughtful participation and to increase attentive focus. Then we consider strategies to refine your reactions to students' mistakes, strategies that encourage participation, and strategies to create low-stress ways of using mistakes for learning.

♣ STRATEGY: Enforce Wait Time

When you plan to call on younger students, even those who don't volunteer, an enforced wait time after the question is asked is necessary to keep overeager classmates from calling out the answer. Use of "engaging challenge" to enforce this wait time serves this purpose. For example, tell students that to be considered, they cannot call out an answer or raise their hands until you say a particular number (for example, a multiple of five, a number greater than today's date, and so on). When you ignore their call-outs and raised hands, because these actions violate the rule, students will realize that they won't be recognized unless they listen carefully and follow all the rules; they must wait for the clue they need to hear before they can answer.

♣ STRATEGY: Call On Multiple Students

You will increase attentive focus among younger children by calling on multiple students to respond to the same question without saying if their answers are correct. Only the person who thinks, learns. When students hear a classmate give an answer and the teacher say it is correct, they have no investment in trying to evaluate the information themselves. However, if the class culture is one in which students know they are all responsible for trying to answer all questions (because you will ask several students for answers before acknowledging the correct answer), they continue to work the question in their minds or on their papers because they have not been "given" the answer by the first person to solve the problem.

After selecting several volunteers to offer their solutions, call for a vote among the entire class. If the remaining students know that they are still accountable for their own answers, they will continue to be invested because they made an active prediction and will want to know if they were right or wrong. This then motivates finding out how to do it correctly in the future.

You can also ask estimation questions in which each student must select an estimate higher or lower than the previous suggestion so they don't just repeat what a classmate said and so they continue to follow along while other students answer.

♣ STRATEGY: Intervene Immediately

It is important to immediately reduce students' stress when they give an incorrect response, especially with students who typically don't participate in class and whom you coax into responding. To provide quick intervention, it helps to be prepared. When students respond to a question in front of their peers, they put themselves at risk, so thank them for any response they volunteer. For example, say, "You took a tough question. Good for you." If the response is incorrect, see if there is some part of their suggestion that is correct, and then restate the question to fit the response before posing the original question to the class in a different way.

You can also say that the student's answer is very close and you want him or her to listen to the ideas of a few other students, think about how to revise the answer, and then you'll *come back to him or her*. Return to this student quickly with a different question, with one that is easier for him or her to address, or with the original question, if you feel that he or she has had sufficient time and exposure to other students' suggestions to think of the correct answer.

You'll probably know by the incorrect answer whether the error was computational (e.g., incorrect addition) or procedural (e.g., addition when the problem called for subtraction). Your knowledge of the student's general arithmetic foundation will inform you if he or she knows how to add and subtract, but the error was made because the student didn't know which procedure to use. What happens next depends on the student and his or her reason for the error. If choosing the correct procedure is a problem for other students, immediate investigation of the cause of the mistakes will be valuable for all.

You can respond with a positive tone of voice and facial expression and say, "I'm so glad you gave that answer. It reminds me that I didn't fully explain that different words are cues that tell us to subtract. In the question that I asked, I said, 'What is the *difference* between 15 and 5?' You said 20 because you added them, and that did give a *different* number than either 15 or 5. Let's revise (or add to) our list of words that are cues for subtraction." Follow this with similar practice questions, with students responding on personal whiteboards or other response devices.

If the student's incorrect answer is indicative of a below-level mastery of rote memory facts, there is little value in using the error for teaching purposes. To reduce distress over making the mistake, give the correct answer and immediately ask a different question that is correctly answered by the student's response. For example, "You said that 5 times 7 equals 30. Actually, 5 times 7 equals 35, but you are correct that 5 times a number close to 7 equals 30. Do you know what that number is, or would you like to call on a classmate?"

If the error is conceptual or procedural about a topic that the class has already mastered, you can say, "I like that answer because it answers another question that I plan to ask later in this unit." Write down the response in your own words, but add something that will make it a "taking-off point" for something that will come up in the following days: "You said that ⅕ is more than ⅓, which fits with the topic of dividing fractions. I'll write 'fraction division' and use your great example as part of our fraction division lesson later this week."

In the next few days, you can give this student some additional coaching and practice work on denominators to bring him or her up to class level.

When you move on to fraction division, remember to return to this point with the question, "Can dividing ever give you more than you start with?" This provides a bit of cognitive dissonance to promote curiosity in the lesson. After the discussion, direct the class to the fractions you wrote down when the student made his or her original mistake.

Write and ask, "What is ⅕ divided by ⅓?" Write the answer as ⅗, circle the denominators, return to the student, and say, "Now we know that larger numbers have different meanings when they are in the denominators of fractions. This brings us back to the question I asked the other day. Let's make a list of what we learned about that question, which I kept up here on the board. When you divide a fraction by another fraction, why do you end up with a quotient that is more than either fraction?"

✤ STRATEGY: Use Estimation and Prediction to Increase Participation

Because older children have more negative feelings about errors, a good way to promote participation is to ask "mistake-proof" questions. These questions are also opportunities for differentiation, because they include options for students who already know the procedure or facts to respond at their level of increasing conceptual understanding. You can ask open-ended questions about *how to solve* problems (rather than to actually calculate answers) or questions that require only estimation or prediction. Putting students in pairs and groups also reduces mistake negativity.

Opening a discussion with a variation of "How can we find out . . ." is a great way to engage students through their strengths. It also allows students to hear multiple approaches and to choose one they find most understandable. An example is, "If we want to give everyone at your table an equal number of raisins from this bag, what could we do?" Hold up a clear bag with too many raisins to count, so students know they are not expected to know a specific answer.

Your question puts the focus on concept and process. Students are reminded not to give specific numbers, because you are looking for *approaches,* or ways to start to evaluate a situation. As in most math discussions, ask students why they think their suggestion might work. Write down three suggestions and let the class evaluate which ones could work. Students can move to corners of the room that represent each of the three suggestions, plus one that represents "none of these." They can work with other supporters of that technique to create evidence and examples, or relate the process they support to other similar procedures.

Estimate. Students often don't take the time to estimate or check their answers, and when estimation is called for, they may first solve the problem, then write a close round number as their estimate. They likely do this because they have never experienced the "here-me-now" value of estimation.

Encourage estimates by valuing them in multiple aspects of math. Give partial credit for reasonable estimates labeled as such on homework or quizzes. Have students start homework in class, but just with estimates. Even if they know the answer without calculating, have them write a range of answers and a reason why their estimate range is logical. These can be shared with the class when estimates are reviewed before the students leave school to do homework independently. Students then have accurate estimates you already approved with which to compare their homework answers to see if they are on target or should rethink the problem.

Predict. Making predictions, like estimating, is a safe type of "risk-taking behavior" that can stimulate the dopamine-pleasure response and encourage fearful or perfectionist students to take chances without the anxiety (amygdala stress) of being wrong. Emphasize that predictions don't have to be right, and that sometimes even the smartest math students make incorrect predictions.

As an example to demonstrate that everyone makes incorrect predictions (and estimations), explain that you will flip a coin and that students should write down whether it will land on heads or tails. Flip the coin and ask students to hold up their predictions if they were wrong. Students can then look around and see that even the "smart kids" made incorrect predictions.

Experiences such as these gradually help reluctant students recognize that incorrect predictions are not signs of ignorance, so they will be more confident in your explanation that predictions are opportunities for the brain to try something out, then take the actual outcome and use that information to make future predictions more accurate.

Students in upper grades, especially Explorers, enjoy building their estimation skills in real-world situations. Map Readers will enjoy the opportunity to see the goal and the sequential steps that will lead them to success. Offer choices whenever possible so students can participate through their strengths. Written instructions or a demonstration can be offered at the beginning, especially to Map Readers, and notes of the process used can be written at the conclusion by Explorers as they describe what they did. All students can select the manner in which they present their ultimate discoveries for assessment and class sharing.

The use of novelty, surprise, and discrepant events to demonstrate the importance of accurate estimations can help students remember concepts. Examples include the following:

- Overfill a glass of water so the water spills onto the floor. After the class has a good laugh, ask them what you did wrong. (*You didn't plan. You didn't estimate or predict how much the glass would hold and when to stop pouring.*)
- Arrive a minute late for class and tell students you didn't estimate how much time it would take to walk to class from your new parking space (or other location).
- Bring a bag with about 10 small, undividable pieces of candy to class and hold it up. With a smile, say that you will be giving one piece to each student. They will surely notice that you did not bring enough and voice that sentiment. You can say, "Well, I didn't count exactly, so how could I know? What could I have done to bring a more reasonable amount?" Guide them to suggest that you could have estimated approximately the same number of candies as students in the class. Just be sure to have the rest of the candy in another bag!

♣ STRATEGY: Create an Estimating Center

Quantity. Create an area in the classroom where you keep containers of the same size that are filled with objects of different sizes. For an extended center activity, children can write down their estimates of how many objects the containers hold. Encourage students to periodically look at and revise their estimates, if necessary, and have volunteers read some of their estimates. When the actual number is revealed, have students jot a note in their journals if they were over or under (perhaps by how many) and why. Fill the containers with different objects and have students do the activity again, making and revising estimates over a certain number of days.

Weight. To build numeracy and estimation skills, an estimating center can have a scale with items to be weighed. The items can be math manipulatives of the same size and weight, or they can be other objects such as old golf balls. Students first lift and feel a one-pound weight and then put it on the scale to see the weight confirmed. They then estimate how many of the designated items would weigh one pound. They can do this by putting them into a bag and using any method they choose, such as holding the weight in one hand or just remembering the feel of the weight. They then weigh the bag and add or remove items until it weighs one pound. Students should keep notes and repeat the activity with different items. Extensions of the activity can have students work with two or three pounds or mix and match objects—tennis balls and golf balls, for example.

Comparisons. Select two boxes or cans of food that weigh 8 ounces and 16 ounces, respectively. Have students hold each as you tell them (or they read) the weights of the containers. Give students a box or can with the weight covered and have them compare the weight of the new package to the weight of the 8- and 16-ounce samples. They can then estimate whether the new item's weight is closer to 8 or 16 ounces. As students become more successful, they may want to predict a more specific weight. Ask them to tell you why they think the new can weighs 10 ounces, for example, and encourage them to respond with, "It is a little heavier than the 8-ounce can" or "It is much lighter than the 16-ounce can, but not as light as the 8-ounce can."

With this estimation-promoting activity (which can easily become an independent activity), students also build number sense by experiencing the relationships between numbers and real measurements and by developing concepts of *more than* and *less than.*

To further develop these concepts, or for challenge work at the center, you can ask students how much they think an item costs. The goal is not for them to know prices, but to develop the concept that larger objects don't necessarily weigh or cost more. If a student predicts that a $3 box of cereal costs $1 and you say "more," he or she may say $2. You say "more" again, and the student will continue giving answers as you direct with "more" or "less" until the correct dollar amount is guessed. Continue this activity with a small can of a costly item, such as artichoke hearts.

Students doing this extension can keep records of the item size and price and repeat the activity with items they select, perhaps because they know they are more or less costly. When they think they know the concept that price is related to both size and value of the item, they can write their discovery in their journal. Let students know that they did something more important than get a correct answer; they discovered a concept—a key that will help them solve many future problems.

Size. Distribute plastic storage bags of the same size, and have students fill the bags at home with their choice of items (e.g., beans, marbles, lemons) in quantities that they are able to count. In class, students each weigh their bags and remove items so all the bags weigh the same amount. Each student then counts how many items in his or her bag are needed to equal that constant weight, such as one pound. Have them add their data (and attach their bags) to a class chart. Then cover the numbers with sticky notes and have students play a game where they guess how many of each item are in a pound. This game can later become an independent activity during center time. Students build or extend the very important concept that size and weight do not always have a direct relationship to quantity.

To adapt this activity for higher levels of achievable challenge, have students work in pairs or small groups with a scale and a variety of objects to put in bags. Options include predicting (estimating) how many objects would equal a given weight and how many objects should be removed or added after each weighing to get the bag as close as possible to the given weight.

This activity can be further extended as students develop the early concept of multiples. Students can make new predictions to reach a new weight, such as two, three, four, or five pounds. Extend the challenge further by asking students to estimate how much each individual item weighs. This activity can take place before students formally learn fractions, but they can communicate in their own words what they predict once they see, for example, that four objects weigh one pound.

✤ STRATEGY: Estimate Weight with Familiar Objects

This is a great "here-me-now" activity. We know our students' backpacks are getting heavier all the time. They already have prior multisensory knowledge about their own backpacks and those of their classmates. They pick up one another's packs to get to their own, or they pass bags to their respective owners. They carry their own when it is heavy and light. This is an object that transcends language and culture in almost every classroom. This estimation activity therefore provides the comfort of familiarity plus personal interest because it is all about the students themselves and their classmates.

Select several backpacks from volunteers who predict that theirs are light, medium, and heavy. Use a scale and have the students weigh their bags, read the number on the scale (with your help, if necessary), and then write the weight on the board under one of the three categories: *Heavy, Medium,* and *Light.* After each bag is weighed and the weight is announced and recorded (providing both auditory and visual input), pass the bag around so each student experiences the tactile sense of what a bag that weighs X pounds feels like.

After the first three examples (one in each category), have a volunteer predict if his or her bag is heavy, medium, or light. The bag is passed around and each student privately writes down an estimation of its weight before the owner weighs it and posts the weight on the list. You may want to label each bag with its weight written on a sticky note. Students can then return to these bags and lift them again to reinforce their sense of what a 5-, 10-, or 15-pound backpack feels like. This step is especially important when students repeatedly make incorrect estimates.

To keep participation up and fear of mistakes down, students' estimates are kept private. The goal is for each student to improve prediction skills at his or her own achievable-challenge level. Keeping private records reinforces the idea that students are working to improve their own skills, rather than to be better than their classmates.

After students finish weighing and predicting the weights of all the bags, they now make charts or graphs comparing the actual weight with their predictions in the order in which the bags were weighed. Several options are available for students at different levels of mastery. Provide below-level students with appropriate comparison charts, while at- or above-level students can choose the style of chart they want to make. The charts should have spaces where students can fill in the weights of each bag. Next to the numbers representing the actual weights are the students' predictions. If they make bar graphs of the data, they should see that the bars on the bar graphs become closer in height as more bags are weighed.

Advanced students can use subtraction to find the difference between their predictions and the actual weights and then plot those numbers on a line graph (from the first to the last bag), with the bag number on the X-axis and the difference between their estimate and the actual weight on the Y-axis. This will also illustrate the trend in accuracy.

When students evaluate their various graphs, they can discuss what trends they find and how they are represented in different graphs. Why do the bars on the bar graphs become closer in height with more predictions, and why does the line on the line graph drop downward with more predictions? Students can go on to discuss what they predict the next three additions to their graphs would look like and explain how they used the trend to predict this outcome.

For homework, students can choose household objects that they can lift and that can fit on a bathroom scale. They replicate the backpack experiment with 5 to 10 objects, graph their predictions with the actual weights, and describe what they noticed about their prediction accuracy as they gained more experience. (Note: Be sure all students have access to bathroom scales before assigning this homework.)

This activity is an opportunity for students to have a positive, fun experience that develops confidence in their estimation ability. They will be more willing to use estimation in future math lessons and activities, and they will be more comfortable participating in class because they see that estimates are "correct" when they are within a range of answers (rather than one specific number). Estimation begins to feel like a safe way to participate. In addition to increasing comfort with participation by recognizing that everyone makes mistakes (that is, their estimates are not always correct), students see that the more they practice, the better they become at the skill of estimating. Another goal is for students to recognize the value of estimation because it helps them see if their answers are reasonable. That "aha!" moment can promote use of estimation for more of their math homework and test questions.

♣ STRATEGY: *Estimate Circumference*

Select classroom objects for circumference estimation and place them in random order. Students work alone or in small groups to arrange the objects in order, according to their prediction of smallest to largest circumference. They then select a small, medium, and large object and use string or a tracing of the base to determine circumference. From these observations, they estimate and then measure the remaining objects, keeping track of their estimates and actual values. Remind students to record the data in the order in which they make their estimates so they can see their prediction-accuracy trend.

As in the previous activities, students use their preferred method of comparing their estimates with the actual measured circumferences and plot a bar or line graph to find a pattern. As you see students progressing, suggest to more advanced students that they take the more challenging approach of making a graph or chart after gathering data from only half the objects. Each student in this challenge then considers how to use the collected data to more successfully estimate the next half. Suggest that students ask themselves the following questions:

- Am I over- or underestimating?
- How can I adjust my next estimates to be more accurate?
- How did the second half of my graph or chart differ from the first half?
- Can I use this same approach and apply it to other classroom objects for additional estimations?

This activity can also be used to estimate and measure the perimeter of squares, rectangles, and even objects with more than four sides; alternatively, students can advance to predicting surface areas to keep the challenge appropriately engaging. You will see the success of these estimation activities as students demonstrate more confidence in taking risks and participate in increasingly challenging discussions as their comfort and achievement levels increase. Your encouragement and formative feedback help students feel supported, safe, and engaged. Students recognize that your feedback is a valuable tool—not criticism—and they appreciate the benefits of using information about their mistakes to improve their future predictions (answers).

Students increasingly experience mistakes as learning tools, which helps them develop a more confident, positive attitude about math and life. Risk taking (estimation), error analysis (charting results), and perseverance in using the error analysis to make revised predictions reward students with the attainment of greater skill and success.

♣ STRATEGY: Lower Risk with Small-Group Practice

When possible, to keep all students engaged in problem solving, you'll want to have a number of students give responses before acknowledging if any are correct. To build confidence so all students actively participate, and to lower the stress if you call on students who don't usually volunteer, peer and small-group practice is valuable scaffolding. Reluctant participants are more comfortable working with a peer as a way to gain confidence about the accuracy of the answers they offer.

Model peer work before you ask students to work together, first by playing both roles yourself, then with a prerehearsed pair of students or by demonstrating with a prepared student partner. This demonstration will show that the nature of pair work is to solve problems independently and then to describe one's answer to the partner for validation or corrective feedback (from the partner or from you). Students need to understand this is not a time to work as partners to reach a solution together. Once the students have independent answers, they can compare. If their answers are the same, even if incorrect, the high-anxiety student will have the safety of knowing he or she was not the only one who made a mistake.

If students in the pair or small group disagree on their independent solutions, they take turns explaining their reasoning and follow the rule that no one interrupts until the person speaking is finished. Eventually, this practice can work up to a higher level of pair teaching, in which the partner doesn't show or tell his or her way of reaching an answer, but rather asks leading questions to guide the partner to reach an accurate solution. Peer preparation before whole-class response time increases comfort, risk taking, and active learning from mistakes.

As an extension, have students do peer reviews of homework or class work before you call on participants, or use peer reviews as test review. Peer comparisons offer another opportunity to increase verbal math communication and confidence as evenly paired students compare answers and try to convince each other why they believe their answer is correct.

Students work best in this situation when they are at the same achievable-challenge level, which reduces the likelihood of one student *telling* the answer instead of listening and guiding the classmate to the correct answer. However, the ability to choose a partner raises dopamine levels and lowers stress, so you may sometimes allow students to select partners. In order for pairs of students at different achievable-challenge levels to work together, it is helpful to introduce the concept of accountability. In other words, both students are accountable to explain how the problem is solved, and they know that either of them could be called upon to do so. If the peer work is for test preparation and the student *learner* achieves significantly higher accuracy on the type of problems reviewed that day, both students ("learner" and "guide") receive extra credit. This places a tangible value on successful peer work and encourages students to take the task seriously.

♣ STRATEGY: Find Multiple Approaches

Multiple-approach problems strengthen risk taking and participation, increase options for achievable-challenge levels, and reveal math to be a creative process. To ensure that students experience the valuable tool of considering several options and using logical reasoning to select the best approach (for their learning strength or for the type of problem), explain that you are looking not for answers, but for ways to solve the problem and reasons why the student finds one of the approaches best.

The first instruction is to write with words or to show by examples at least two different ways to reach a solution. Depending on the level of achievable challenge, some students may have time for or awareness of only one approach. The strategy still works in their favor because, while others are writing about at least two approaches, those students won't feel rushed. Let them know privately in advance that they are not under pressure to find multiple solutions this time because their current goal is mastering whatever procedure or concept they are at in your extended goal plan.

Tell the class, "This time I don't want you to tell me what the actual answer is. Just tell me what you could do to solve the problem." After students describe their approaches, ask for other approaches without indicating which are correct. To keep everyone engaged, let students discuss the approaches they understand or agree with, and when the different approaches are tested for accuracy, the conversation can continue as they talk about why one approach works better for them.

For example, if the problem was to find the answer to 8×6, students may suggest three options: memorizing the multiplication table for 6, knowing that $8 \times 5 = 40$ and adding another 8 to equal 48, or adding a column of six 8s. Allowing students to personally choose among approaches all confirmed as correct and to support their choice will increase their comfort levels. This process also builds math logic, intuition, and reasoning skills that extend into other academic subjects and real-life problem solving.

Another example might be to ask students how to find out which fraction is greater: ⅖ or 3/7? Encourage students to draw diagrams or to use any math tools in the room (e.g., manipulatives, rulers, graph paper). The answers are likely to match the learning strengths of the students. Explorers may use three manipulatives that are each ⅐ of the same whole and compare the size to two ⅕ pieces. Map Readers may draw two equally sized circles or rectangles on graph paper, divide one into five parts and the other into seven parts, color two and three sections of the respective shapes, and then compare the two colored regions.

Students who have mastered a higher conceptual level of equivalent fractions may find common denominators. Other students who understand that fractions represent division may divide the numerator by the denominator and find which quotient is larger. Other options include making two number lines so students can fairly accurately divide one number line into seven sections and another into five sections. Students who are comfortable with estimation may evaluate which of the two fractions is closer to one whole.

With the large number of options, and a problem in which an exact answer is not required, students come to realize that if they can't remember a particular rule, they can create their own system of comparison. This approach also reinforces for students the benefit of knowing supporting concepts so they don't get stuck because they can't remember the algorithm—a memorized procedure they can reproduce but don't necessarily understand. The important message with multiple-approach problems is that participation is not limited to the students who are faster or always correct, because you emphasize the value of the different ways of approaching the problem, not just the solution. If a student devises an appropriate method to reach a solution but makes an arithmetic error, he or she can still be recognized for the accuracy of the reasoning. You can take this method, demonstrate how it works perfectly when the subtraction or addition is corrected, and prove it by using the method to solve a similar problem with different numbers. The student who suggested this method will feel the dopamine reward of a correct approach because he or she realizes that that approach can generate lots of correct answers. The student has discovered a concept or creative idea that belongs to him or her and is a useful tool.

✤ STRATEGY: Use Problems with Multiple Correct Answers

Problems with multiple correct answers are fun for students to work on individually or in pairs, then in small groups where they explain their different solutions to their classmates. This approach lowers mistake negativity because students know they can use their learning strengths, strategies they recall, and rote facts they remember, and then check with a partner before sharing with the class or group. These problems also provide for achievable challenge because students who find one way are instructed to keep going and find as many variations as they can. This gives students who need more time the comfort of knowing that they won't be the last to finish.

For example, a game called "This Is Not a . . ." encourages multiple solutions and is played in a relaxed environment that encourages creativity. Students pass around an object—such as a toy telephone—and say, "This is not a . . . ." Younger students name an object that is not a toy telephone (for example, "This is not a pencil."). Older students continue and say, "This is not a toy telephone, it is a . . . ," and they gesture or mime to suggest the object that they are pretending the toy telephone is—perhaps a computer mouse or a hair dryer. The gesturing students can eventually name what they are pretending the object is, or classmates can guess. Games such as this one help students become comfortable with a certain amount of ambiguity and gain the confidence to speak up when appropriate.

The most important learning activity in math, or any subject, is participation. This naturally leaves one open to making mistakes, but the brain learns by restructuring neural networks that make incorrect predictions. Playing this game lets students participate without the fear of making a mistake, which gradually builds confidence to participate, even if the response is wrong.

♣ STRATEGY: Learn from Mistakes

One of the most effective ways to help reduce students' fear of making mistakes is to model the process of how *you* learn from your mistakes. You can then progress to demonstrating how students can learn from errors you purposely generate, and when students are prepared to reflect on, not react to, mistake negativity, they can be guided to learn from their own mistakes.

Strategies in this category aim to lower the emotional overreaction the brain has to mistake negativity; to help students discover the motivating memories of perseverance, including perseverance through mistakes; to build students' tolerance for mistakes; to reduce excessive anxiety-related errors; and to encourage students to strive for achievable challenge. These strategies, and your modeling, help students understand the value of mistakes.

Start a discussion with a statement or question such as, "Does a guitar player prefer playing songs with chords only after mastering dozens of chords?" Then promote discussion of personal memories of mistakes that led to success and gratification: "Can you describe a time when you kept trying even though you felt like giving up?" "How did you learn to play soccer so well?" "Do you still enjoy the beginner snowboarding runs now that you are advanced, or do they seem boring?"

This discussion will remind your students that once they built up their skills in playing sports, a musical instrument, or video games, it became boring to stay at the same level—*but they made mistakes as they took on challenges to advance.* Gradually, with effort and practice, they made fewer mistakes and enjoyed the pleasure of doing something with greater skill. When they make the connection to math challenges, students come to understand that mistakes are a natural part of new skill development in math just as they are in mastering a new video game or an athletic skill.

You will reduce your students' fear of making mistakes when you help them understand that when they feel disappointment or embarrassment from mistakes, *their brain is working well, and the rewiring that's occurring will lead to a smarter brain for future answers.* For example, an error recognized in homework or during class participation may be disappointing, but without that response, the brain would not be stimulated to reprogram the faulty information pathway, and the same mistake will be made again.

Making mistakes in front of others is stressful for most students, yet correct understanding is constructed as much from recognizing mistakes as from rote rehearsal of procedures. The most brain-friendly environment is one that encourages participation and corrects the assumption that making errors means you are not smart. A positive, growth mind-set can become integrated into the class culture by using the strategies in this chapter to increase participation, reduce mistake anxiety, and build students' confidence in the brain's great power to grow smarter from mistakes.

5

Change Your Intelligence?
Yes, You *Can!*

Every man can, if he so desires, become the sculptor of his own brain.
—Santiago Ramón y Cajal

When I went to medical school and became a neurologist, I didn't know that I'd eventually become a teacher and write about teaching strategies that are based on brain research. Eventually, the connections between my two professions became clear, but it wasn't until a few years later that I realized that my students would benefit from understanding how their brains learn and could use that knowledge for self-empowerment.

Your students probably came to your class assuming that learning math quickly was a sign of natural, unchangeable intelligence and that they could not change the brain they inherited. Such an assumption can have far-reaching implications: students who believe learning mathematics is strongly related to innate ability show less persistence on complex tasks than peers who believe that effort is more important (U.S. Dept. of Education, 2008).

Children, as well as many adults, mistakenly think that intelligence is determined by genes and that effort will not significantly change their potential for academic success. Especially when students believe they are "not smart" and nothing can change that, the realization that they *can* literally change their brains through study and review strategies is empowering. I see this same sense of empowerment develop in my neurology patients who have lost function due to brain disease or trauma. Through practice—beginning with visualizing movement of the paralyzed limb, or imagining themselves speaking—patients regain function. The neuroplasticity of the brain enables the construction of new neural networks as undamaged areas take over the jobs previously performed by the damaged regions.

Learning About the Brain

Students are motivated to take action as they learn about neuroplasticity, see brain-scan evidence of brain changes, and see the results of their own actions when, with more and more practice, *neurons that fire together, wire together*. They quickly learn that stimulating a neural circuit that already holds information makes it stronger.

♣ STRATEGY: Teach Lessons from the Brain Owner's Manual

In the realm of educational mandates that tie test scores, not progress, to school funding, students believe that right answers are more valuable than questions or understanding. The result can be a loss of children's natural curiosity and enthusiasm and eventually, for some, an increased sense of futility and boredom such that they begrudge their time in school and resent homework.

Teaching your students lessons from the Brain Owner's Manual (Appendix B) adds to their confidence that they can change their math ability and intelligence overall. Increased understanding of how the brain learns leads to increased control over their own learning and increased motivation.

The Brain Owner's Manual gives educators information they can use to show students how their brains learn, remember, and grow. Armed with this knowledge, children recognize that they can choose how to develop their brain wiring, attention power, and memory, and they can set goals they believe are achievable because they learn that they can change their intelligence and reach desired potentials.

When teachers guide students through the brain, they give them the gift of motivation and optimism. Children understand that homework and brain-friendly review change their brains because *practice makes permanent,* and mental muscle builds just as their body's muscles build with exercise. Students also enjoy learning about their most fascinating organ and are delighted to discover that they have the power to be as smart and skilled as they would like to be—in school, sports, performing and visual arts, and social situations.

At the beginning of the year, I like to ask my younger students if they think they can change their brains. I show them fMRI scans of brains before and after people learn to juggle or play a musical instrument. My students see the increased density of brain cell connections and activity in the places in the brain that control muscles and coordination responses used while juggling or practicing the piano. This visual evidence leads them to conclude that yes, they *can* change their brains.

To dispel notions that effort is useless because they are only capable of the intelligence with which they are born, I tell older students that humans have between 30,000 and 40,000 genes—only 10,000 more than a worm— and ask what that fact might mean about heredity versus environment. When students understand how their brains learn, they are motivated to take action.

I teach my upper-elementary and middle school students about the brain filters that determine which information reaches their higher, thinking brain (the prefrontal cortex) and how they can consciously influence those filters. They learn about changes in their brains that take place through neuroplasticity. I show them brain scans, and we draw diagrams and make clay models of connections between neurons that grow when new information is learned. I call their lesson summaries "dend-writes"—a play on words because, as the students have learned, a *dendrite* is a branchlike structure that extends from a nerve cell. We discuss how more dendrites grow when students review information and have adequate sleep. I even send home electron-microscope pictures that show growing dendrites and synapses and assign students to explain that aspect of neuroanatomy to family members and then report their responses.

I use analogies from sports, dance, and music instruction in discussions with students about how they build greater skill the more they practice a basketball shot and how their guitar or ballet performances improve the more they rehearse. Then we make connections to explain that their brains respond the same way when they practice their multiplication facts or reread confusing parts of a book, because, through neuroplasticity and myelination, practice makes permanent. (Myelination is the process in which a thickening coat of insulating myelin wraps around the most active axons. Myelin increases the speed of information transmission along the connections between neurons and the efficiency of retrieving the information stored in that neural network.)

My students are particularly excited about the "RAD" systems in their brains. They learn about the reticular activating system, the amygdala, and dopamine, and they have opportunities to discover that their effort and focused attention determine what information gets into their "thinking," reflective brains. For example, they discover the increased recall of historical events that can result when they have been guided to visualize or dramatize those events.

When students are struggling, you can explicitly remind them that the brain grows stronger as a result of effort and practice, and that over time and with continued effort, understanding the material and solving the problems will get easier. When students understand that, through neuroplasticity, their practice makes permanent, they develop motivation for studying and practicing.

The following quotes are comments made by students after their first semester, during which I sprinkled my lessons with "syn-*naps*" (a strategy explained in Chapter 6) and "dend-*writes*" and incorporated "neuroscience" instruction into their math classes.

> I imagine neurons making connections in my brain when I study, and I feel like I'm changing my brain when I learn something, understand it, and review it.
>
> —Emily, *7th grade*

> If I use my prefrontal cortex to mentally manipulate what I learn, my dendrites and synapses grow and I will own that learning for a long, long time. I won't have to learn fractions all over again each year.
>
> —Cory, *7th grade*

I *can* be smarter. If I focus, practice, and use my strengths I can grow the brain connections and cement the memory circuits to be smart. And the more I practice, the stronger my connections become, and the smarter I am. It feels so good to know I have the power to be smart. I also discovered that when I grow those dendrites and synapses, learning seems easier and I don't get lost in class.

—Mitch, *5th grade*

I didn't know that I could grow my brain. Now I know about growing dendrites when I study. Now when I think about watching TV or studying my notes and correcting my homework mistakes, I tell myself that I have the power to grow brain cells if I do the work. Even though I want to watch TV, I make the decision that I'll do the work so my brain grows smarter. It is not always fun, but I know it works, so it's worth it.

—Page, *8th grade*

To get an idea of how these techniques really changed how my students study and learn, I kept track of the students who maintained good records and wrote or said the most compelling comments about how their brain knowledge encouraged or empowered them. I asked their other teachers for copies of their grades from before and after they completed their Brain Owner's Manual lessons. It was certainly not a controlled experiment, but the results are worth noting. Students who expressed positive feelings about their abilities to change their brains did, in general, improve their grades, turned in complete assignments with more regularity, participated more in discussions, and were more likely to ask for help to find out what they did wrong on tests or homework in my class and in other classes.

♣ STRATEGY: Discover "How My Brain Works Best"

Have students create their own Brain Owner's Manuals to represent their understanding in ways that make sense to them. Various activities can help make brain processes tangible to younger students. For example, the class can hold hands in a circle and act out the roles of electrical impulses traveling through connecting axons (their right arms) to the neurons (their bodies) and then on to the next axon (through their left arms). Alternatively, they can then make clay models or draw diagrams of dendrites, synapses, and axons.

GRAY MATTER

Neuroplasticity

The loss of vision has been associated with better performance on nonvisual tasks, such as touch sensitivity and sound localization. Research evidence suggests that these gains are linked to the recruitment of the visual cortex, which normally functions only in response to visual input, to process nonvisual input.

To study this hypothesis, researchers (Merabet et al., 2008) put normally sighted individuals into a state of complete visual deprivation for five days and immersed them in an intensive tactile Braille training program. Following the five-day period, blindfolded subjects performed better on a Braille character discrimination task than the (nonblindfolded) control group who received the same Braille training.

In the blindfolded group, serial fMRI scans revealed an increase in brain cell activity within the visual cortex in response to tactile stimulation. This increase in signal intensity was gone 24 hours after the blindfolds were removed. Research suggests that complete visual deprivation in normally sighted individuals can lead to profound, but rapidly reversible, neuroplastic changes by which the visual cortex becomes engaged in the processing of nonvisual information.

The speed and dynamic nature of the observed changes suggest that the visual cortex has the potential for other functions—in this case, touch—and these normally inhibited or masked functions in sighted people are revealed by visual loss. The unmasking of these pre-existing, unused networks shows that they may become active when needed, and possibly develop into permanent circuits if the visual loss is sustained (Merabet et al., 2008).

Instead of sending home a typical beginning-of-the-year letter about having a quiet place to do homework and other standard bits of advice, I have students experiment for themselves. I assign homework for the first few weeks and include specific conditions under which they are to do the homework. I ask students to nominate items for this list. The usual conditions are these: with and without music, with and without text messaging, taking frequent snack breaks, taking planned exercise breaks, working in bed or at a desk, doing homework early or late, studying all at once or reviewing small sections at a time. Each day, students write the time they start and finish their math homework (parents help younger students), what variable condition they changed, and how they do on a short quiz of questions pulled right from the homework the next day. They collect their own data and compare their findings with those we collect as a class. They add the data to their own Brain Owner's Manuals and write their own letters home about the best homework conditions for themselves and for the rest of the class. The following excerpts are a few examples from actual students' letters.

> I experimented and know I focus better, finish faster, and remember more if I don't send text messages or watch TV when doing my homework. I know I need to schedule syn-*naps* (breaks every 20 minutes for 5 minutes) to refresh my dopamine. Now I even get the hard problems right because I don't get frustrated the minute I don't understand something. It works at home and now it works on tests.
>
> —Randi, *7th grade*

> Before I begin paying attention, I try to filter out distraction, so my RAS [reticular activating system] picks up the important information.
>
> —Gabe, *8th grade*

> I imagine neurons making connections in my brain and I feel like I'm learning something. Every time I think of not studying I think, no, my brain won't form new connections.
>
> —Mario, *5th grade*

Reducing Negativity by Improving the Classroom Environment

Earlier chapters in this book have described a variety of specific strategies to reduce negative attitudes toward math and to help students build more confidence in their ability to succeed in math. Here we consider some additional strategies that focus on the broader classroom environment, with the goal of creating a favorable setting for "changing brains" and improving intelligence. They include practicing relaxation techniques; using humor, visuals, and stories; and creating positive teacher-student relationships.

STRATEGY: Practice Relaxation Techniques

It is beyond the scope of this book to describe the many helpful activities you can use with your class to help students develop skills of self-calming and focused alertness. You'll find a number of such activities that I developed through my work with the Hawn Foundation on their Web site (www.thehawnfoundation.org). Even simple activities such as taking time to teach and practice diaphragmatic breathing, using imagery to reduce anxiety, and having students recall one of the happiest days of their lives before tackling math problems or tests will show results.

STRATEGY: Insert Humor, Visuals, and Stories into Math

To insert humor into mathematics in my classes (and thus increase dopamine levels in students' brains), I use narratives, draw pictures, or put up humorous math-related cartoons, such as those from *What's So Funny About Science* by Sidney Harris (1977) (many of which are math-related).

In an earlier book, I described my corny but memorable sketches of a pot hanging from a noose, used to help students remember the word *hypotenuse* (pot in a noose), and the drawing of an open and closed polygon with a bird, Polly, escaping from the open polygon ("Polly gone"). I make up narratives about the numerator and denominator of a fraction racing to buy a house for sale at a great low price. The long-division symbol represents the house. I explain that the numerator has the advantage because he is on top and gets a running start. He gets to move into the house, but the denominator stops outside the front door.

Using narratives to explain mathematical concepts resonates because it relates to the structure of stories that children have heard their whole lives. The presentation of the information is familiar, evokes positive memories, and is easy to follow. Studies show that information presented as stories is rated as more interesting and has higher content recall than the same information presented in other types of text or verbal formats (Britton, 2008).

Have fun and give your students, especially Explorers, a chance to get creative and bizarre with drawings that represent math terms. Post these drawings on the board for others to enjoy and learn from, and give the "artist" (especially if he or she is not a great math student) a chance to have his or her creation proudly displayed. Keep these sketches or narratives for following years, so that new students can enjoy seeing what the "big kids" drew and wrote when they were in your class.

♣ STRATEGY: Create Positive Teacher-Student Relationships

When students are questioned about their reasons for dropping out of high school, they often mention teacher-student and adult-mentoring relationships. Teachers and students in grades 1 through 12 were interviewed about what characterizes a caring, responsive relationship that leads to a productive learning environment. Common themes were teachers who use clear communication about high expectations, offer support, answer questions until the student understands, treat students with respect, use students' names and greet them in and out of class, and appear happy and enthusiastic about what they teach (Brown, 2003; Comer, 1993).

It is not easy to conceal your frustration when students appear not to care or try, but realize that in the brain-stress state, students who have developed math negativity as a result of past experiences don't have the resilience or motivation to invest effort in trying again. It is not useful to blame previous teachers; instead, understanding that the negativity has built up over time helps you recognize that the goals you set need to be achievable.

What can you do in the short term and the long term to rebuild students' math attitudes? First, keep in mind that students processing input in their reactive brains (fight/flight/freeze) are responding without conscious choice. Recognize that when students misbehave or are disruptive, they are simply displaying the brain's involuntary response to frustration, stress, and anxiety. Consider the possibility that failure to do homework may not be the result of laziness or disrespect; rather, from the student's viewpoint, it may be less stressful to accept the consequences of incomplete homework than to do homework and risk being called on for answers that they are afraid will be incorrect (Walker, Colvin, & Ramsey, 1995). Start with a positive attitude, demonstrate confidence that your students can achieve their appropriate challenge levels, differentiate instruction, work with students' strengths, and motivate by taking account of students' interests. Soon, through your own neuroplasticity and with time and practice, you will be the kind of caring, responsive teacher students say they want.

You must also be conscious about the negative feelings you may have for some students and take care to respond to them with the behaviors associated with positive student-teacher relationships. Use encouragement, speak respectfully, keep your facial expressions upbeat, maintain eye contact, and use students' names when you greet them in and out of class.

Pay attention to your inadvertent behavior to these students—such as offering shorter explanations to their questions or providing less wait time because you feel you have adequately explained the topic. Avoid patronizing them with overly enthusiastic responses to basic questions that are below their level of achievable challenge.

Your optimism, enthusiasm for math, and demonstration of your expectation that they can succeed will motivate your students' positive response. Help them recognize their strengths, not just in math skills, but also in group collaboration, attempts at participation, and willingness to ask questions and make corrections. Encourage them to recognize and repeat successful strategies and acknowledge their achievement of defined achievable challenges.

Here's what learning without negativity sounds like in class, as expressed by two 7th grade students:

> The one thing that's really neat about math now is I'm not afraid to try new ways to solve problems or say what I think in a class discussion, even if I'm not sure. I'm not so panicked, so I actually can focus on what my classmates say in the discussion and that gives me more ideas. I remember times I asked the teacher for help but was so nervous about the teacher or other kids thinking I was dumb, that I didn't even remember the

explanation. Now I'm calm enough to listen and really hear what I need to not be confused.

I found out that with effort I could build more nerve cell connections, which means I have stronger math memory. I can snag information I stored in one category, like learning about decimals, and apply it to something I need to do, like figure out money. I never believed in myself, and now I'm not surprised when I do well and I am excited to keep working, even when I make mistakes, because I don't think there are limits to the goals I can reach.

Retraining the Brain by Reducing Stress

If students worry about making mistakes in class or on tests, the resulting stress can cause the amygdala to shunt brain activity to the noncognitive lower brain and prevent the information processing from taking place in the prefrontal cortex. Singing a song, reading a familiar poem, doing a stretch or short dance routine, watching a humorous cartoon, taking a few deep breaths, or thinking about a favorite place can lower stress and increase the flow of dopamine to set the positive emotional mind states that keep information flowing to the *reflective* instead of the *reactive* neural networks. These interventions to reduce stress also increase the brain's ability to inhibit distractions (Hopko, Ashcraft, & Gute, 1998).

✤ STRATEGY: Lower Stress While Increasing Class Participation

Anxiety takes up working-memory space because the prefrontal cortex diverts resources to deal with emotional distress. With less working memory available, students have decreased capacity to retrieve stored memories they need in order to calculate or solve problems. Think of the list of things that elevate dopamine, such as humor, optimism, positive experiences, and choices, and use these to promote the increased positivity, perseverance, and memory that accompany increased dopamine.

Remind students of the individual strategies they have recorded as being helpful in their attempts to do their best work, such as writing down important formulas or hard-to-remember computations and keeping the information on their desks during discussions of the topic. They won't have to worry about remembering them once they start answering a question—and that means there is one less stressor to block amygdala flow to the prefrontal cortex.

Writing down the steps to a solution, even when students can do a process mentally, is important for students with high levels of math stress, because once written down, the information does not have to be held in working memory. This simple task will give them more confidence to answer questions in class, especially when you request that students explain their reasoning.

Preview the Material. Some students, especially ELLs or students with exceptionally high math negativity, will go right into a state of high stress each time a new topic is introduced in class. One way to effectively deal with this situation is to explain to students (and their parents) the concept of "priming," or previewing material to "prime" the brain for receiving new knowledge. You can suggest that the night before a new unit will be introduced in class, especially one with new math vocabulary or symbols, students spend a few minutes at home reading the introductory pages in their text. Explain that the idea is not to try to understand everything they read, but just to have some familiarity with the new words, symbols, or procedures. Previewing the next day's lesson in the book reduces automatic anxiety because students come to class prepared with at least a small amount of background familiarity.

The 10-Minute Stress Buster. As mentioned earlier, both mistake anxiety and the stress of lessons above or below students' level of achievable challenge increase negativity, shift the brain into fight/flight/freeze mode, and decrease higher-order thinking. This stress-buster strategy can be used throughout various lessons, especially during direct instruction, the introduction of new concepts, homework, or test review.

We already know from evaluation of effective teaching strategies that frequent assessment and corrective feedback—occurring every 10 minutes or so and conducted in an emotionally supportive manner—are powerful tools that promote understanding and long-term memory and develop the executive functions of reasoning and analysis. Using individual whiteboards for active participation is a low-stress, high-engagement strategy because students are showing you what they know without having to say their answers out loud—and all students participate, not just the few who answer verbal-response questions. The other benefit of this frequent assessment is that it provides the information you need to support students at their appropriate levels of achievable challenge throughout the lesson. With this strategy, students know that if they begin to experience boredom from prior mastery or frustration from confusion, no more than 10 minutes will go by before the situation will improve.

To reduce mistake anxiety, have students write responses to your frequent questions and briefly lift their whiteboards for you to see. You can respond with a simple nod, acknowledging that you noted their response. The process prevents classmates from seeing one another's responses because the boards are held up for only a brief time, and classmates are busy writing their own responses. This is not initially formative or corrective feedback, but as you'll soon realize, it becomes such as a result of the stress-buster intervention. (For some students, based on your knowledge of their skill level and level of comfort with mistakes, you can devise a signal—such as a "half nod"—to indicate an incorrect response. This would be helpful for students who finished the calculation early and can then use the remaining time to redo the problem while other students finish their first attempts.)

If many students make errors in their whiteboard responses, you have received feedback indicating that you need to reteach the information in another way or readdress background knowledge. When most students answer several sequential questions correctly, write the answer and continue instruction without a lengthy explanation of how to solve the problem. Students who are bored from a previously mastered topic are relieved, and the students with incorrect solutions know that within the next few minutes they will have individual help to address their confusion.

✛ STRATEGY: Use an Individualized De-stress Technique

Among its long-term, goal-related attributes, one characteristic of formative assessment for learning is that it occurs while there is still time to take action. The 10-minute stress buster is not for detailed corrective feedback. Your intervention is intended to reduce frustration or boredom immediately, taking only a minute or two of class time without breaking the flow of instruction.

Preparing students for this de-stressing technique takes about 10 or 15 minutes of explanation a day for about three days, but once students understand and practice their roles, the process runs smoothly. The following description is the longest part of the process, and you may need to read this twice, so have a drink of water, stretch, think of a funny story, then read on.

You should prepare students for this system when you describe achievable challenge so they know that, depending on the topic, some students will be ready to move ahead, some will need more practice, and some will need more foundational knowledge before they can follow along with the lesson. During the de-stress technique, you will give each student a quick cue that lets him or her know what to do next. The goal is to resume the formal lesson with all students back in their comfort zones, engaged at their appropriate challenge levels. Depending on the grade you teach, you will have a wall chart with either pictures or sentences to guide each student to the appropriate activity they will do when you resume instruction or practice after the de-stress technique.

Students who repeatedly answer correctly and don't need more practice with the topic are directed to the "Moving On" chart instructions that include some consistent options that require no explanation and new options that are related to the lesson or unit topic but follow a consistent pattern and don't require detailed explanation. Younger students can be prompted to do independent work, such as independent book reading or computer programs. The students whom you direct to the "Moving On" chart will not continue listening, discussing, or practicing the lesson in progress (at least not for the next 10- to 15-minute segment, until they are de-stressed) because they know they will not suffer the frustration of repeated drill on something they already know. Instead, they will participate in higher cognitive or conceptual exercises that can include partner discussion (in a quiet corner of the classroom) or independent work such as responding to the following prompts:

- What other math process does this remind you of that you learned before, and why might it be useful to know how to do this math? Write your ideas in your math journal.
- Make up a problem similar to the ones you just did, solve it, and trade with your partner. Solve each other's problems, and if you don't

agree, explain your reasoning to see if you reach agreement. Hand in your work.

- Go through the notes you took on the lessons this week and compare with a partner to fill in things that he or she has and you want to include. (*This is also a good option for the entire class while you walk around and give each student his or her plan for the next class segment.*)

When students get a majority of the questions wrong, and you know they have been struggling in math due to low foundational knowledge, language differences, or processing difficulties, there isn't time in these brief de-stressing interventions to provide the math remediation they need. However, you can immediately lower their stress by a code word or phrase that reminds them what they will do for the next lesson segment and of the options you offer for help outside of class time when they will have the opportunity to learn the topic at an appropriate pace. This important immediate intervention is designed to get these students out of the fight/flight/freeze state they are in due to frustration or confusion, so at least *some* of the input in the rest of the lesson reaches their prefrontal cortex and their behavior remains under conscious control.

When I know from a student's responses that he or she does not have the necessary skill to follow the next part of the lesson, I smile and say kindly, "Flowing River." Early in the term, I establish these "code words" with students, and they know that I will use these phrases if I decide they are too confused to understand the next part of the lesson. The "code words" are quietly said to individual students as I walk around the room.

My typical explanation of "Flowing River" is usually something like this:

I know you are confused and frustrated. I will work with you in [*fill in the predesignated time here*] so you will be ready to work with the class tomorrow. But for the next 10 minutes, when we take what we just finished to a higher level or do more practice problems, don't try to figure out every step or follow all the details of the explanations and become more frustrated. Let the new math vocabulary words, symbols, or procedures flow over your brain like a river carrying seeds. Even without understanding everything and doing the practice problems, your brain will take in some of the things we say and write. If you are not stressed about trying to solve the problem, your brain will still get something from listening. When we meet later, those little seeds left by the flowing river will sprout in your brain. They are the beginnings of the new brain networks you will build as your understanding grows. Your job is to watch and listen, keep calm and open to what you hear, and not worry about what you don't understand.

When you create your own version of "Flowing River" and an appropriate explanation, you have the tool that keeps your students from acting out or retreating to the fight/flight/freeze mode. The result is that students watch and listen, and they are not anxious about being called on or worried that you will scold them for not solving the new problems. In this state of the "Flowing River," the input can get through the amygdala into the prefrontal cortex, where some parts of what the students see and hear will leave a memory trace. These traces will be activated when the student hears them again during remediation. The side benefit is that the student's reactive brain will not be directing his or her fight/flight/freeze behavior to act out in a disruptive way. This tool works more and more successfully as students experience for themselves how this priming does, in fact, make it easier to learn the material when they meet with you later.

As you probably noticed, the "Flowing River" activity is similar to the strategy described earlier where students preview an upcoming lesson even though the information might not make sense. Both strategies are effective because the brain is more receptive to input that has already been viewed or heard, and research has documented the positive effects of this approach. In a study of previewing, words were presented to subjects at a speed faster than they could be consciously read or repeated, yet when the subjects were shown the words later, they identified the previewed words faster even if those words were presented in a different font, case, or size (McCandliss, Cohen, & Dehaene, 2003).

For students who demonstrate moderate success with their whiteboard assessments, the de-stressing break provides a few minutes for them to go back to questions they got wrong. If you leave the questions on the board with the correct answers, students can take advantage of the time when you walk around the class to work alone or with a partner to try the problems again. When the lesson resumes, these students will continue the directed learning, discussion, and whiteboard practice with you. You can also add questions such as "How did you figure that out?" so the responding student gets the benefit of reinforcing his or her new learning through verbal communication, and classmates in this continued-practice group (and the "Flowing River" group) have the opportunity to hear about the process in new words that may make more sense to them than the ones you previously used. Students are less anxious about participating out loud because the group remaining in the lesson is smaller and consists of individuals at a similar level of achievable challenge.

There are two additional de-stress activities you can use during this break. At the beginning of the term, have students draw question marks and light bulbs on index cards that they tape to their desks or math notebooks. If students have a question they are embarrassed to ask in class, they flip over the question card. You can then check in with them later so they can ask the question privately. If the question can be answered clearly in a short time, the break provides time for that. If, however, a question merits more attention than you can give at the moment, give that student a cue that indicates his or her question is important and you will address it during a designated help time.

The bright idea light bulb card is useful for students who frequently want to share lots of personal information related to the topic or who want to describe the way their father taught them to do a problem. Some children find it very stressful not to make their comments immediately. They can't regain focus on the lesson due to their frustration and concern that they will forget what they wanted to say. Flipping the light bulb card relieves their anxiety once they know that they will have an opportunity to share. Indicate this with an agreed-upon code that you will either begin the next section with their comment or listen to it in detail during de-stress time or another designated time.

Building Confidence by Constructing Missing Foundations

Convincing students that they can change their brains is easier when they have at least a minimum level of confidence in their abilities. The following strategies are ways to bring students up to the class level of foundational knowledge through independent, paired, or parent-assisted practice or by providing scaffolding for them to use during lessons, homework, and tests until they learn the background information and prior knowledge needed to progress with the class. These strategies include errorless math, cue words, and calculators and tables. A final strategy deals with students who need help building self-reliance because they worry that their foundational skill—or other knowledge—is somehow lacking.

♣ STRATEGY: Ensure Success with Errorless Math

Errorless math is a foundation-building memory tool especially useful for students who are reluctant to take on *any* challenge because of negative experiences with math. The goal is to build math confidence along with the required facts. Errorless math uses time delay to motivate children through their own successes in achievable challenge. In this system, teachers or peer-tutors provide verbal or gesture prompts to increase the probability of a correct response, which eventually becomes the correct answer (Bender, 2005).

The traditional way multiplication facts are practiced in class is by having students see how many multiplication problems they can do on a worksheet in a set amount of time. This is a high-stress activity with a low reward because students have no motivation to review the facts they got wrong or try the ones they didn't finish.

In the delay method of errorless math practice, students build speed and accuracy in a high-success, low-threat, appropriately challenging activity. An example is the use of flash cards to practice multiplication facts. Here are step-by-step instructions:

1. Prepare a list of the calculations from the flash cards on a sheet of paper. These can be on a template, with multiplication facts at the appropriate level pulled and copied for the student. On these forms, include three columns next to each multiplication question, labeled "correct repeat," "correct wait," and "correct response."
2. Start with review and confidence building. For example, show the question $3 \times 4 = \underline{}$ on the card and without any delay say the answer. The student repeats the question and answer, just as you said it, while looking at the card (visual and auditory memory stimulation). He or

she then turns the card over to confirm that the answer is correct (positive reinforcement/dopamine pleasure).

3. Place a check in the "correct repeat" column for the student's proper repeating of the calculation.

4. If the student doesn't repeat the math fact with you correctly, read it again and have him or her repeat it correctly with you. Don't write anything on the list until he or she does the correct repeat, and then check the appropriate column. Continue with the next card. Limit the number of cards to an achievable-challenge number, determined by your observation of the student's attention span, and always include several cards the student has already "mastered" in previous sessions.

5. Delay step: After enough practice, when the student seems familiar with the math facts on two or three cards, simultaneously show the card and read the question together but *wait about three seconds* to see if the student jumps in with the answer *before* you say it. If he or she is successful, turn over the card to confirm his or her response. If the answer is correct, make a check in the "correct response" column of your list.

6. If the student doesn't jump in during the brief delay, proceed as before and say the answer. He or she then repeats the original question and answer before turning over the card to confirm accuracy. (Mark the column as in Step 3.)

7. If the student waits through the delay for you to say the answer and then repeats it correctly along with you, check this as a positive response in the "correct wait" column. Check this column because the student knew to wait and then said the correct answer with you. The practice continues to be errorless and nonthreatening because it acknowledges both correct waits and correct responses.

   • The process is almost completely errorless because if the student says the correct answer, that is a correct response, and if he or she waits for you to say the answer and then repeats it, that is also a correct response.

   • If the student makes an incorrect response by giving an incorrect answer, there is no box to check for "incorrect response." Leaving the blank space for that problem on the list gives you a record that the problem was missed *without visible negative feedback to the student*. There is, however, immediate corrective feedback because you ask the student to try again. On the second try, you say the problem and the answer without any delay, so the student won't jump in with an incorrect answer, and he or she will have the opportunity to repeat the correct answer. Having your notes open and visible to students throughout this process is part of the positive experience. To reinforce motivation and positive math attitudes, you can also show students a record of their increasing mastery for "correct wait" and "correct response" as practice sessions continue.

8. Provide verbal or gesture cues to increase the probability of a correct response. For example, if a student is multiplying numbers with decimals and forgets to count the number of digits following the decimal points in each multiplier, say the word *decimal* if he or she appears to be finished and has not placed the decimal in the product. In that way, the student will not actually make the error in the final answer he or she writes down. Even though a cue was needed from you, the student ends up writing a correct answer and benefits from both the practice and the pleasure response from the achievement.

Students who appreciate errorless learning may also enjoy practicing with a recording of math facts that has pauses before each answer. You can record your own or purchase them from Web sites listed in Appendix A. Parents, aides, and responsible classmates can take over as coaches in errorless math once they observe the process and are adequately trained.

Because multiplication is an early "make-or-break" foundational skill—at least until fractions rear their heads—it is useful to have several approaches to instruction. Start by building the concept that multiplication of whole positive integers is the same as adding the same number a certain number of times.

Instead of having your students practice multiplication tables in the order of 1 to 10, use the dopamine boost of choice and encourage students to start with the ones they like, or guide them to see how much multiplication they already know by starting with 1, 2, 5, and 10. They can count by 2, 5, and 10 to get most of these correct.

Give students copies of the multiplication table of facts through 10 and have them cross off the ones they have mastered. (You can print these, individualized for achievable challenge, using templates such as those available at the SuperKids Web site: www.superkids.com/aweb/tools/math.) Once students have the 1, 2, 5, and 10 columns crossed off, have them find these numbers in the rows of other numbers. Keep their spirits up as they cross off the "doubles" they now know. For example, if students know how to multiply by 5, show them that they already know both $3 \times 5 = 15$ (in the row for multiples of 3) and $5 \times 3 = 15$ (in the row for multiples of 5).

After students master the remaining multiplication facts with errorless math, they have the pleasure of crossing all the numbers off their chart. Remind them that the brain still needs exercise, just like muscles, to stay fit. Explain that to keep their new neuron network strong, they need to periodically activate the networks, like charging a cell phone to keep it working.

When these facts become automatic and your students start solving problems without taking time to calculate a multiplication fact, remind them that their efforts paid off. They now have the mental muscle they need to solve many new problems that require this foundational information, including problems involving division, fractions, and decimals.

♣ STRATEGY: Understand Cue Words

Students need to know common math symbols before they can follow a mathematical procedure. Because many words are used to indicate the common symbols, especially in word or story problems, students can keep individual and whole-class charts with words that are represented by the signs for *multiply, divide, add, subtract, equals,* and *ratio.*

Eventually, students will encounter more than one meaning for cue-word phrases, such as "*How many* raisins can each student have?" The "how many" can be a cue for division, addition, or subtraction. Let students know in advance that cues are not rules, and they can't turn off their brains and automatically substitute a plus sign each time they see or hear "how many." It helps to write examples of all cue words that might be associated with sentences, calculations, and symbols. These examples will be particularly helpful for the multiple-meaning cue words:

> **Addition:** *add, plus, sum, total, altogether, increased by, grew, gained, total of, combined, more than* (as in, "3 *more than* 7 is 10"), *put together, in all*
> **Subtraction:** *minus, take away, difference, less than, from, remove, subtract, gives away, sells, loses, fewer than, decreased by, difference between*
> **Multiplication:** *product, times, doubled* (*tripled*, etc.), some problems give information about *one* and ask for *total amounts* (also, when dealing with multiplication of fractions, *of* usually means to multiply)
> **Division:** *quotient, percent of, per, ratio, division, separated into, cut into, divided by, shared equally by,* some problems tell about *many* and ask about *one*
> **Equals:** *comes to, is, totals*

♣ STRATEGY: Use Calculators and Tables

As we know, working memory has limited storage. Working memory is the memory you use when you keep numbers in mind while you do mental math, such as $83 - 17$ or 14×11. We all have different limits to the amount of information our working memories can hold while we proceed with a calculation. Students do not need to memorize every foundation fact before they can understand the key concepts (Bransford, Brown, & Cocking, 2000).

Consider how you might lower the barrier (not the bar) for students who haven't mastered multiplication facts but are ready to move on with the class to division. In this situation, multiplication calculation would likely slow them down, and they would grow frustrated or not have the working memory to do the multiplication slowly while following along to learn the concept and procedures of long division. For example, given the long division problem $428 \div 7$, a student not yet at automaticity in multiplication facts might spend five minutes adding up a column of seven 6s to find that $7 \times 6 = 42$. By the time he or she is finished with this step, the class will be onto the third step of the problem, and the student won't be able to catch up. It is frustrating for students to be held back because of gaps in basic arithmetic while they are learning a new operation. When introducing a new concept that depends on foundational automaticity, calculators or multiplication tables are a reasonable scaffolding tool.

Students can use a calculator or a multiplication table taped to their books or desks while practicing long division. They will still practice and do homework that builds their multiplication automaticity, but they will not miss out on progressing to the new skill (i.e., division) with the class. The intrinsic reward of understanding the new concept along with their classmates helps motivate these students to continue working on the missing foundation instead of falling further behind, which would increase their math negativity.

In a study of the use of calculators to increase math attitudes and achievement, researchers found that without calculators, students have minimal opportunities to engage in and actually use what they learn in a meaningful way and feel that they are always *catching* up instead of *keeping* up. The researchers recommend that when a calculator makes the difference between math motivation or alienation, its use is reasonable. Students can and should develop the deficient arithmetic skill facilities that result in their need for the calculator, but it is more desirable to fill in missing skills than to reverse alienation (Hembree & Dessart, 1986).

Multiplication-table charts may be sufficient for students with good spatial orientation and visual tracking skills. Students who respond to the visual sequence of entering the numbers and seeing them on the calculator screen benefit from the visual-spatial sequence of entering 4, then 6, and seeing 24. It is beneficial to have students try both options and keep records of their multiplication progress to see if their memory is better with the sequence of numbers on the calculator screen or with the consistent patterns of the multiplication chart.

✤ STRATEGY: Build Self-Reliance

What about your students who frequently worry that their answers on class work are incorrect and want you to check each problem before they continue, or those who call out, "I don't get it" before you've even finished an explanation or example? These students need to build self-reliance and confidence to replace their learned helplessness. It helps to have a set policy that students follow before they ask for help.

To encourage this kind of independence in class, I ask my students to do two things before asking me for help. First, they must find a solved example in their text or class notes that is similar to the problem they are working on. Next, they are to carefully read and follow the example so they can explain it to me in their own words. Often, they are able to connect the process with the new problem with very little help from me. Many students become self-sufficient at this process, and their math confidence grows along with their skill.

If a student has become very insecure about his or her math skills as a result of negative school experiences, it may be more difficult to wean him or her from asking for help before trying to work independently to solve a confusing problem. When this occurs, be reassuring and uncritical as you remind the student that you are confident he or she knows what you are going to suggest. Often, the confidence this student gets from your support as he or she looks for similar examples in the text, class notes, or previous homework will be enough to persevere independently and gain the associated intrinsic reward. It is truly one of the most rewarding teaching experiences to see a student arrive at an "aha!" moment that accompanies a transformation from the predictable "I don't get it" to "I did it! I found an example and figured it out myself!"

The strategies described in this chapter all support the physical act of neuroplasticity, so whenever possible, remind students of how much you believe in their brains' power to change and get stronger. The great thing about using strategies that correlate with brain research is that students enjoy and are empowered by learning that they can recognize changes in their brains as they gain knowledge, correct mistakes, participate, and persevere.

Don't hesitate to repeat descriptions of neuroplasticity, especially when students are stressed by a skill they think is not and will never be within their abilities. Remind students that each time they review or repeat information or an action, there is activation of their nerve cell circuit. Reinforce their understanding that each time they activate a circuit (because they call it into active memory to solve a problem, answer a question, or practice a movement from sports to keyboarding, for example), the electric current flowing through that circuit signals the brain to make that circuit stronger.

Your encouragement and the neuroscience you share from the Brain Owner's Manual in Appendix B will continue to help students recognize how they have the power to change their brains, make them remember longer and stronger, build skills by practicing, and build their memory banks by reviewing. You can even adopt a class motto of *Practice Makes Permanent* so your students are frequently reminded that, with effort, they can succeed because they have the power to change their brains and intelligence.

6

Motivating All of Your Students

....

> A #2 pencil and a dream can take you anywhere.
> —Joyce Myers, *American businesswoman*

You are patient, offer encouragement, provide time during and outside of class for students to receive extra help, and differentiate for achievable challenge, yet some students still repeat the same complaints we hear every year, from "Math is my worst subject" to "I already know that. Can't we learn something *new* this year?"

Because *boring* is the most common word students use to describe the reason for their math frustration, it helps to consider what students mean by this. The power of boredom or alienation goes beyond not enjoying a specific course or subject. It leads all the way to dropping out of school.

Nationally, 50 percent of high school students in the largest U.S. cities disengage completely by dropping out. This is the highest dropout rate we've ever seen. It is the first time since the institution of public schools in the United States that it is more likely that students' parents will have graduated from high school than for the students themselves to graduate. The United States is the only industrialized country in the world where this is the case. Many students who don't drop out nevertheless disengage through inconsistent attendance, disruptive behavior, and inadequate homework and test preparation (Organization for Economic Co-operation and Development, 2004). Another study found that math failure starting in 6th grade and an unsatisfactory behavior mark in at least one class before high school were two of the four greatest predictors of dropping out of high school. In fact, 75 percent of students with these records as early as grade 6 dropped out of high school (Neild, Balfanz, & Herzog, 2007). The association of failure in math and unsatisfactory behavior is a natural consequence of the fight/flight/ freeze reaction of the brain to math negativity.

Surprisingly, it is not the difficulty of academic content that drives students to drop out. In 2006, 81,499 students in grades 9 through 12 from 26 states participated in a survey of student engagement and reasons for dropping out. Only 27 percent said they would consider dropping out because the work was too difficult. The majority of those students suggested that the reason they would consider dropping out was that school was boring. What did the respondents mean by "boring"? The reason 74 percent gave for being bored in class was that the "material wasn't interesting" and 39 percent stated that the "material wasn't relevant to me." Also important is the level of interaction between teacher and student, with 31 percent attributing their boredom to having "no interaction with teachers" (Yazzie-Mintz, 2007).

We strive to motivate students so they are successful in math and develop the extended skills of reasoning and analysis that accompany true conceptual knowledge of mathematics. In addition to keeping them from dropping out, motivation has other benefits. Motivated students are the most responsive and least likely to be "behavior problems" because, as just mentioned, math negativity is associated with the reactive fight/flight/freeze behavior. With your intervention, students' attention and positive attitude can replace negativity.

The strategies in this chapter start with a focus on capturing your students' collective imagination and attention—exactly what is needed to get information to the prefrontal cortex instead of being conducted to the fight/flight/freeze area of the lower brain. We will then explore strategies to sustain this attention and construct working memories by lowering stress and increasing positive emotions.

Motivating Students Through Active Engagement

Knowing your students' interests and background knowledge helps you create lessons with sensory input that is most likely to be selected by the RAS. Because the RAS responds positively to sensory input predicted to increase survival, cause pleasurable feelings, and result in achieving immediately

GRAY MATTER

The RAS

All information enters the brain as sensory input, and all such input must pass through the reticular activating system (RAS), the brain's most primitive filter, to enter the information-processing areas. Billions of bits of sensory information are available every second from sound, light, color, smells, touch, position of muscles, and our internal organs. Only a few thousand of these can get through the RAS each second (Lawrence, Ross, Hoffman, Garavan, & Stein, 2003).

If it weren't for the RAS filter, our nervous systems would be overwhelmed by input. Instead, the RAS—and later, the amygdala—allows the brain to establish priorities and select what is valued enough to admit into our perception. The RAS's selection determines what the thinking brain has to work with at a conscious level. If the information in your lesson is not selected by this primitive filter, then it doesn't have any chance of being "learned."

In animals, including humans, the RAS is attentive to changes in the environment and selectively alerts the brain to new sounds, sights, or smells that may indicate danger or opportunities for pleasure. Those selections allow the animal to survive (food, water, and safe habitats are deemed pleasurable) and the species to be sustained (the sensory input related to a potential mate is selected for its association with pleasurable sexual experiences). Our RAS has not evolved much beyond that of other mammals—it remains alert first for potential danger. Once the RAS establishes that nothing has changed that requires instant protective reactions (fight/flight/freeze), it then selects sensory input about changes that are associated with previously pleasurable experiences.

The RAS response to sensory input affects the speed, content, and type of information that enters the higher-thinking regions of the brain. The RAS is key to arousing or "turning on" the brain's level of receptivity to input. For example, PET scans show increasing activation in the RAS as people change from a relaxed state to an attention-demanding task (Kinomura, Larsson, Gulyas, & Roland, 1996).

Cognitive studies show a correlation between intelligence and the ability of the brain to select which patterns of information pass through the RAS. Students vary in their ability to effectively inhibit task-irrelevant sensory input. In one study, children with high intelligence employed more constructive matching of information to task goals and more effective inhibition of task-irrelevant information compared to a control group of "average" students, suggesting that the "high-intelligence" children's RAS filters more efficiently select input based on the goal or task at hand (Vigneua, Caissie, & Bors, 2006).

desirable goals, using strategies that stimulate a "here-me-now" response increases the likelihood that this primitive brain filter will select the information you want your students to take into their brains.

Because the RAS also looks for change in the environment, surprise and novelty can be valuable classroom tools for promoting attentiveness in students. Novelty can be incorporated into lessons through variations in sensory stimuli (tone of voice, volume, or rhythm); visual cues or changes such as color and movement; or other tactile or kinesthetic changes. All of these cues can call attention to what you want your students to see and hear. Your sensory input needs to be selected by the RAS as more potentially pleasurable than the sounds coming from the playground or a conversation with the classmate in the next seat. That's pretty stiff competition when your job is to teach long division.

♣ STRATEGY: Engage Students with RAS Grabbers

Novelty, change, and surprise (the unexpected) engage students' attention and can promote a state of eager motivation (Hunkin et al., 2002). Telling students they must learn math to pass tests—or even because they need the knowledge for future success—is not sensory input valued for selection by the RAS. That information on its own does not have the "here-me-now" qualities that the RAS connects with survival or pleasure.

What *will* engage the RAS at the start are things that incorporate change or novelty, evoke curiosity, or are associated with pleasure. You can grab your students' attention with movement, color, music, advertising, discrepant events, or things that don't behave in expected ways (such as your walking around the classroom backward before starting a lesson about negative numbers).

Knowing that novelty is a big RAS motivator, it is neuro-*logical* to conclude that if the sensory input is not novel enough to get RAS attention—such as lessons that move too slowly for those who already know the information—it will not engage students' attention. Individualized instruction that is mindful of different levels of achievable challenge once again becomes important. For example, when some students already know the content and their RAS tunes out, they may miss information that is actually new and important when it comes up. These are lessons that require intermittent short segments of instruction in foundational knowledge (which you know will be "boring" to some students) but that soon include new information these students don't know. Plan ahead with some agreed-upon cues (e.g., put on a cap, write in a special color) or code words so these students will alert their RAS to refocus attention when you reach the new, important material that comes up in the lesson.

The following are some additional examples of how to build novelty into learning new information.

Speaking Voice. Try speaking in a novel accent or a different cadence of speech.

Suspenseful Pause. Pausing dramatically before saying something important will build anticipation as the students wonder what you will say or do next.

Word Order. Start your sentences with an unusual word order, such as with verbs first, like "Yoda-speak." For example, to begin a lesson about *order of operations*, say, "Think, you will when solving math problems." Extend the interest by putting up a problem for which students need to know the order of operations to reach a correct solution, such as $80 - 20 \times 3 = \_\_$. Some students will answer 180, and others will appropriately multiply first and find 20 for the solution. Now students will *want to know what you have to teach them* because the answers are so different, and it is likely they were all sure their answers were correct.

Color for Novelty and Differentiation. Write key points in priority colors and have students use pencils or pens in the same colors in their notes. If you choose green, yellow, and red to show increased importance, you can have a picture of a traffic light in the classroom to remind students of the system. Not only will the change of color increase RAS attention, the movement in the room as classmates pick up new pencils refocuses the attention of students who have zoned out. Students will also have cues of importance when they study and want to fill in missing information for words they wrote in priority colors.

Font. Changes in fonts (including color) can revitalize focus on tests and assignment sheets.

Thinking Cap. Wear a special cap for important lesson points and rotate it to the side and then backwards to emphasize higher and highest priority.

Play a Song. When students enter the class, play a song that relates to the lesson and challenge them to figure out what the correlation is between the song and the lesson. They will listen to the lesson more carefully and pay attention in order to make the song-lesson correlation.

Clothing Cues. Wear clothes with geometric prints for lessons on shapes.

Estimation Motivation. Overfill a water glass; assign extreme numbers of homework problems; let students out late for recess. When they question you, respond that you did not estimate before you planned.

Radish. Put a radish on each desk before students enter. Don't tell them why, but challenge them to write down their ideas about how the radish relates to the lesson as the instruction proceeds. You can relate it to almost any lesson, such as a topic that begins with an *R* (ratio, rate, or radius) or an activity in addition or subtraction where students in groups combine and remove radishes to get sums or differences.

♣ STRATEGY: Reinforce Achievable Challenge with "Friendly Numbers"

Most children enjoy the achievable challenge of video games and are intrigued when they see a person do math as quickly as it could be done by a calculator. An example would be a unit about "friendly numbers," such as mentally adding $23 + 27$ by changing the numbers to $20 + 30$ to find the sum of 50. You can write the problem on the board while students use calculators to find the sum. While they punch in the numbers, you'd announce the solution before the answer comes up on their calculators. To prove that you didn't just memorize that one problem, you can give the students a list of friendly number problems, and they can take turns selecting the one for you to do mentally while the class does it on their calculators. After the lesson, they can complete the list for class work or homework.

Students are motivated to learn how you were able to come up with the answer so quickly. Their primitive brains are curious, and this opens the gateway for them to *want to learn what you have to teach.*

GRAY MATTER ⚙️

Novelty and Attentive Focus

In an experiment to evaluate the influence of novelty on attention, subjects were shown a variety of photographs followed by a series of words to sort according to meaning. The next day, one group viewed new images and the control group viewed familiar ones. They were all then asked to recall as many words from the previous day's list as they could. Recall was significantly better in the group that had just viewed new images. In the research team's opinion, novelty seems to promote attention and memory. To improve memory, they suggested starting lessons with surprising new information before moving on to new instruction (Eriksen & Schultz, 1979).

♣ STRATEGY: Build Curiosity and Positive Anticipation

In addition to opening the RAS to new input, lessons that are punctuated with positive anticipation, curiosity, and evident connections to previous positive experiences also increase dopamine levels for pleasure, focus, and memory. Some approaches that serve this function make use of advertising techniques, discrepant events, and surprising calculation results.

Posters. Build curiosity about an upcoming lesson with posters giving hints about the topic—a form of "teaser" advertising. Students can write down their predictions and will enter the class with curiosity each day to see if you've added another clue. For example, a fraction lesson can be advertised with hints conveyed by pictures of an arm in a cast one day, an X-ray of a fractured arm a few days later, followed by sheet music with whole and half notes, and finally desks arranged in a new way (half on one side of the room, a quarter in another section of the room, and two-eighths in another section).

Discrepant Events. Start a class or unit with a demonstration that has an unexpected result or with a statement that is counter to students' first intuition. This grabs their attention by creating *cognitive dissonance,* and their minds note a discrepancy between what they see or hear and what seems logical to them. From the students' desire to clarify the disconnect—between what they think they know and information that doesn't seem to fit with their prior knowledge—comes eagerness to move to a new, higher level of understanding. The following are some examples of discrepant events with instructional value.

Volume. Have students fill tall, thin containers with water or beans and then predict if all the water will fit if it is poured into a shorter container (which you selected because it has the same volume). Showing that a tall, thin glass tube can contain the same volume of water as a wide, shallow bowl can provoke the curiosity that motivates interest about perceptions of volume. You are providing a puzzling and interesting challenge and motivating focus when you tell students the explanation will come to them as they learn the day's mathematical procedures and concepts.

Multiples. Pose this question to your students: Would you rather get one cent a week doubled every week starting now, or each week receive one dollar for every year of your age?

Fractions. Have students predict which is larger—half of a quarter of a pizza or a quarter of a half of a pizza. When they are then told the amounts are equal, you can connect their curiosity with a lesson about multiplying fractions.

Size and Mass. How many cotton balls will fit into a glass jar of water filled nearly to the brim before it overflows? Because students don't realize that the balls are mostly air, many more fit than they predict.

Ratio and Proportion. How are we alike? How will the ratio of your height compared to the circumference of your head compare to the ratio of the same measurements of your classmates? You can use these questions to introduce the concept of the "golden ratio."

Graphing for Prediction. Before a lesson on graphing on X- and Y-axes for prediction of a trend or rate, ask students how many drops of water will fit on top of a penny before water flows off the edge. The number will be larger than they expect because surface tension allows a dome to form. Ask them to see how many drops are held on a nickel and a quarter and graph the results to predict how many will fit on a half-dollar.

Circumference. Using the overhead projector to demonstrate, ask students what will happen if two quarters are placed flat, side by side, face up, and then one is rotated around the circumference of the other. (The quarters should be fairly new so that the edge ridges are not worn to keep them from slipping during the rotation.) Ask these questions: If the portraits on the two coins are facing in the same direction at the start, how will they be aligned at the end of one rotation? How many times will the portrait on the rotated coin go around in one rotation? Logic suggests that the portrait on the rotated quarter should go around once and end up in its original position after the rotation. After doing the activity, most students experience cognitive dissonance because what they thought was logical is not correct. The rotated quarter actually makes two complete rotations around the stationary one.

As these examples suggest, the success of discrepant events is evident when students are surprised and want to know why the event or calculation turned out not to match their expectations. Once you have students involved and interested, they are highly motivated to satisfy their extreme curiosity. Once again, *they want to know what you have to teach!* The value in all discrepant event activities is not to discover the phenomenon. The goal is to come up with valid reasons for why the event happens. *Students do not learn by simply doing activities, but by thinking about what they discover.*

In many discrepant-event activities, students can do a quick inquiry in small groups, starting with a plan that will provide evidence for the reason they predict. They then make observations, collect data, analyze results, make adjustments based on the results, and ultimately reach a conclusion that resolves the discrepant event and their previous misconceptions.

✤ STRATEGY: Avoid Negative Reactions to the Unexpected

Lessons that include surprising phenomena or information can create a stimulating learning environment in which brain states of disequilibrium-prompted curiosity are strong learning motivators. Several considerations will help you avoid *negative* reactions to discrepant events.

Especially among young children who have unstable lives away from school, the unexpected can signal danger. Students whose common state of mind in math class is bewilderment may be pushed beyond their stress

GRAY MATTER

Cognitive Dissonance

When students are aroused (but not distressed) by disequilibrium-prompted curiosity (i.e., cognitive dissonance), their RAS is alert for environmental and sensory cues that will restore equilibrium. They are attentive for information to solve problems or to understand the demonstrations that provoked their curiosity. They are motivated to follow the day's lesson because they can't evaluate the situation with the information they start with. This reaction is related to the primitive instinct of animals to evaluate change first for survival, then for potential pleasure in response to the unexpected in their environment. (An example would be a fox coming out of its den and seeing and feeling snow for the first time.)

In the brain, the amygdala is positively stimulated so it can transmit data efficiently from the sensory-response centers to the patterning and memory regions. The hippocampus, where relational memories are encoded, is primed to bring up any previously stored information that may potentially connect with the new data to bring a solution and restore equilibrium. In the hippocampus, if incoming sensory information differs from stored knowledge, it sends a pulse of dopamine to dopamine-holding regions of the brain stem. From these regions, nerve fibers extend back to the hippocampus and trigger the release of more dopamine. This feedback loop in response to novelty is why we remember things better when they appear in a novel context.

level with the added confusion of cognitive dissonance. If you anticipate these situations, consider preparing these students in advance with assurance that although something unusual or confusing will take place, it will not be bad; their classmates will also be confused and you will help them learn what it means.

Plan to avoid quick fixes, such as students who understand the seeming incongruity announcing the explanation for the entire class. Use tools such as whiteboards so students have a way to let you know that they "know." They can work with peers on an extension of the concept or develop their communication skills by working with students who remain confused even after the class has determined the explanation.

The goal of the cognitive conflict is not only to capture students' attention, but also to promote critical thinking and build conceptual understanding. Instead of confirming or denying students' explanations, ask questions or propose "what if" scenarios to encourage students to arrive at explanations on their own.

Sustaining Motivation Throughout a Lesson and a Unit

Once you've grabbed students' attention and used strategies to promote entry through the RAS of the sensory input related to the math lesson, you still need to sustain motivation for the remainder of the class period (as well as over the course of however many class periods the unit requires); you also need to keep stress down so information continues to get through the amygdala to the prefrontal cortex. Now is the time for strategies that relate lessons to topics and experiences that students find meaningful and relevant (connecting to prior knowledge), offer choices, use "syn-*naps*," and incorporate physical movement into lessons.

♣ STRATEGY: Make Connections Relevant to Your Students

Textbooks often start new units with a "real-world application" that may be interesting to a mature brain with neural circuits that have experienced pleasure from knowing the related math, but sometimes students cannot connect to the application. For example, students in math classes may love pizza, but perhaps they haven't had experiences to establish the networks that directly link learning measurements of pizza ingredients with the pleasure of pizza. Thus, using a description of how to use measurements to make pizza will not be valued at the unconscious level of the RAS. Pizza is pleasurable to eat, but young students may have no pathway in their brains that directly links learning more math with the pleasure of pizza. That connection comes when they are older and the prefrontal cortex has matured to have enough top-down control to "tell" the RAS that the information about measurements involved in making pizza is valuable and will lead to pleasure.

Real-world connections to future jobs are also too remote to signal the RAS that the math knowledge is valuable at the "here-me-now" level at which the RAS works. It is unlikely, for example, that most students' RAS cares if archeologists use scientific notation for carbon dating.

Your lesson openers will be the most successful when they connect with other parts of the unit and are perceived as invitations for students to enjoy a new, positive, *personally* valuable experience. Your opening is really a presentation to the RAS. The big picture needs to get through the primitive gatekeeper that gives priority to novelty, threat, and pleasure and that *sustains* curiosity.

For young students, relevant real-world connections to estimation might include watching in surprise as you overfill a glass while talking to them. When they tell you that your water is spilling over, this is your chance to say, "Oh, I should have estimated how much water this glass would hold." Students can then guess how much water different paper or plastic cups will hold before pouring water to check the accuracy of their estimates. After this exercise, have students brainstorm a list of things that are important to estimate, such as doses of medicine or equal shares of water when it is scarce.

✤ STRATEGY: Use Openings That Sustain Curiosity

Consider big opening questions, surprising facts, media presentations, meaningful current event connections, or guest speakers who can relate the topic to the "here-me-now" level of students' primitive brain filters. These connections need to be very obvious so the value of the upcoming math is directly linked to the prediction of imminent pleasure. Once students are "hooked" on a topic, they will be motivated to listen, participate, and learn for the duration of the lesson and the unit.

Your own learning outcome or goal for the unit is usually to add to foundational knowledge and help students make new connections and extensions to their core math concepts. This outcome is part of your big picture for the school year. Keep in mind that to succeed at that goal, your opening is the time to prime students' motivation and build enthusiasm for activities you've planned to appeal to their varied learning strengths and interests. Once you have the students engaged, you can build on the positive connections and curiosity you ignite to achieve your goal successfully with your motivated students.

In your planning, consider what you most want students to know and then work backward to develop an opening that promotes sustained interest toward that goal. If possible, represent the unit in several different ways that appeal to different learning strengths and levels of achievable challenge so you can continually engage all students.

Here are some fascinating facts you can use as "big openings" with your students to help them with number sense, specifically with understanding large numbers:

- One billion seconds is almost 32 years.
- One billion eye blinks (each eye counted separately) occur during an average human lifetime.
- One billion grains of salt fill a bathtub.
- One billion words are heard and read during a lifetime.
- Three billion heartbeats occur during an average lifetime.

The following suggestions are additional strategies to open a lesson in a way that sustains curiosity.

Big-Picture Previews. Initial big-picture connections to a new topic activate prior knowledge, stimulate personal interest, demonstrate real-world "here-me-now" value, and guide students to develop personal goals that will keep them connected to the content. Students will show that they are authentically engaged when they start making personal connections and asking questions.

Before a lesson on negative numbers, bring in different objects that relate to negative numbers, such as a thermometer, a photo of a ship above and below water, a SCUBA tank (or a photo of a SCUBA diver), a checking account register, or stock market quotes. Students begin by considering what the items have in common and move to the idea that things can be "less than one." This will develop an interest in the topics you'll teach as students connect with the goal of learning about negative numbers. The multiple big-picture items can then serve as opportunities for students to choose personal reasons why they would consider negative numbers useful.

Engaging Opening Questions. Questions that engage curiosity and interest can be great openers. The best questions for sustaining interest are planned to help students discover the big idea of the unit; they compel students to seek answers as you help guide them in the search. These are questions that can't be answered without the information you need to teach, but they are interesting enough that students stay alert for clues that bring them closer to an answer as the unit progresses.

For example, to lead a lesson about fractions, ask younger students, "Are there any numbers that are more than 0 but less than 1?" Older students are naturally curious about questions that seem illogical or impossible. Therefore, you can begin a lesson on fraction multiplication with the question "Can you make numbers smaller by multiplying them?"

Another benefit of curiosity-provoking questions is to build students' perseverance through longer and more challenging uncertainties. A 3-year-old child doesn't have the executive function of delay of immediate gratification to wait until the end of his or her birthday party to open the gifts, but as children get older, they usually enjoy the anticipation of seeing the gifts displayed and increase in number because they have experienced the pleasure of positive expectation and the reward of opening all their gifts at once.

♣ STRATEGY: Create Unit Titles

Instead of using the unit title from the textbook, have your students work in small groups to think of and nominate unit titles every few days. At the end of the unit, they can vote on a class title or select the one they prefer for their own journals. Discussing possible titles activates prior knowledge, reinforces big ideas, and increases the connections between new information and stored memory as neural networks grow.

Near the conclusion of the unit, to further reinforce newly embedded learning, students can choose to keep their identified titles or change them. Then, for the positive motivation that accompanies choice, students can write a paragraph, song, or poem or draw sketches to communicate why the title suits the big idea of the unit. The final unit title, similar to an analogy, builds a connecting bridge for future access to the stored memory when the students want to retrieve the knowledge.

♣ STRATEGY: Use Syn-naps to Maintain Motivation

We know that *synapses* are the gaps between neurons in the brain. What I call "syn-*naps*" are brain breaks that restore neurotransmitters depleted when the same neural circuit is used for extended periods (as few as 5 to 10 minutes for lower-elementary students). They also keep the amygdala from getting overstressed. It is not surprising that students need these syn-*naps* more frequently during math than during most other subjects. During these breaks, the newly learned material has the opportunity to go beyond working memory to be consolidated into relational memory in the hippocampus while students replenish their supply of neurotransmitters in one circuit and use another neural pathway for a new activity.

The syn-*naps* offer an opportunity to regain students' wandering attention because they involve a change of some sort (type of activity, new partner, movement), but these three- to five-minute brain breaks do not need to disrupt the flow of learning. Sometimes syn-*naps* can be as simple and brief

GRAY MATTER ⚙

Highly Focused Students and ADHD Students

Sometimes stopping for needed breaks is particularly difficult for students who are very intense in their focus or highly interested and invested in an activity. Just as artists in the midst of painting or athletes and actors in the "zone" of peak performance may disregard their bodies' cues to eat or sleep, students engaged in their cognitive "zones" need your guidance before dopamine and serotonin depletion leads to frustration and even anger.

On the other hand, some students with attention deficit hyperactivity disorder (ADHD) have limited reserves of neurotransmitters to maintain focus and may experience the decreased cognitive efficiency of mental fatigue even sooner than their classmates.

as singing a math song or hearing a math joke while students stretch or get a drink of water.

When selecting an activity for longer syn-*naps,* consider math games that are fun and competitive but safe, so students will feel comfortable playing (lowering amygdala stress) and want to play again (inducing dopamine pleasure). Other kinds of syn-*naps* activities may continue with the same math topic but use a different neural-processing system, such as providing different sensory input when you go from discussion to manipulatives, from individual to group work, or from a demonstration to a workstation activity. The following are examples of various syn-*naps* activities.

Buzz. An example of a low-stress, win-win game is Prime Number Buzz. Students stand in a circle or at their desks and go around the room in order, saying either the next sequential number if it is a composite or "buzz" if it is a prime. If they are incorrect, they sit down, but they keep listening and when they catch another student's error, they stand up and rejoin the game. (The same game format works for Multiples Buzz, using multiples of, for example, 3, 4, and so on.)

Telephone. This is a variation of the perennially popular Whisper Down the Lane. Students line up in two teams and play with a math vocabulary word and definition. The last person in each line recites the words she heard, and the team closest to the correct original definition wins the point.

Commercials. Students work in small groups to create a commercial to advertise a math "product" by showing why it is valuable. For example, if they choose to sell the operation of division, their advertisement would promote the value of division. "Have you ever had 10 cookies to share with 5 friends? If you buy our product called 'division,' you'll be able to figure out how many cookies to give each person so everyone gets a fair share."

Pick a Card. This activity uses two identical decks of cards, each containing a number of cards equal to the number of students in the class. Deal out one deck of cards (one card to each student) and keep the other deck. Ask a math question and then pick a card from your deck. The student with the matching card answers the question; if this student doesn't know the answer, he or she consults a "team member" (another student with a red or black card, or one who has a card of the same suit) who volunteers to help him or her answer. When doing this activity, more students actively think if you ask the question *before* selecting the card that designates who will give the answer. Selecting the card first might stop others from thinking about the answer because they know they do not have the matching card.

Who's Who in Math. Students give a short biography of a mathematician or teach a minilesson they prepare and share with the class.

Code Breaking. This activity provides practice in finding patterns. Examples such as "S M T W T F S" (first letter of the days of the week) are available in math activity books.

♣ STRATEGY: Add Movement to Syn-naps

Dopamine, serotonin, and norepinepherine—neurotransmitters that affect focus, memory, and mood—increase with exercise. Students evaluated on standardized tests taken after moderate exercise were more successful than students who took tests after 20 minutes of sitting still (Hillman et al., 2009). Because movement is another RAS-alerting stimulus, you can incorporate movement in several ways to keep students on track.

Brain Shake-up. Toss a ball (I use a rubber brain ball available through brain-toy Web sites) from student to student for math review. The student who catches the ball says something he or she remembers from the just-concluded discussion or comments about what message he or she got from a guest speaker. Another option is for the student who tosses the ball to ask the receiver an appropriate mental math question. To adapt this to a class with very diverse levels of math students, classmates can play on teams standing on opposite sides of the room. The receiver can have the option of asking a team member for help, but the receiver must ultimately give the answer. Alternatively, each receiver can request a Level 1, 2, or 3 question for a suitable, realistic challenge. You can help the questioner adapt the question so that it is appropriate for the chosen receiver.

Have I Got Something to Tell You! Students are given note cards with math-review information, such as a multiplication fact or, for older students, a procedure to explain, for example, "When subtracting a positive integer, the answer comes from moving to the left on a number line." Students then walk around the room and share their math facts or explain their procedures to several classmates. If students are unclear about their particular math facts or procedures, give them another card or encourage them to ask for help. The listener repeats the fact or reasoning (in his or her own words) before the students switch roles and repeat the process. The cards can be saved and used another day, with students receiving different cards each time. To keep track of which cards they have had, students can write their initials on the cards they use.

Simon Says. This game is easily adapted for math instruction. For example, you can tell students, "Make an acute angle with your arms" or "Make a semicircle with your fingers."

And in This Corner . . . Students move to different corners of the room in response to questions. For example, ask, "What kind of angle is this?" Students would then move to Corner 1 if the angle displayed is *acute,* Corner 2 for a *right* angle, Corner 3 for an *obtuse* angle, and Corner 4 for *uncertain.* The uncertain students can then walk over to classmates in the other corners and ask for their reasons until they decide which is the correct answer.

We've Got Something in Common. Students stand up and meet with two different classmates and try to find something they have in common, such as names with six or more letters, a birthday on a date that is a multiple of 5, or three or more colors in their shirts. Another movement option has students read and explain their "dend-*writes*" (summary of the previous day's math lesson), listen to their partners, then add missing information to their own summaries before finding another partner and repeating the process.

I'm No Ordinary Zero. The *Human Place Value* unit from the *Surescore/ MARS Math* series of math activities uses a Human Place Value Chart you make by dividing a piece of butcher paper the length of the classroom into 14 sections (or fewer for lower grades). Label each section, starting from the left side: ten billions, billions, hundred millions, and so on, down to tens, ones, tenths, and hundredths. Make sure you include a decimal point between the "ones" and "tenths" sections. After students review place value concepts, such as each section of the chart being equal to ten times the section to its right and one-tenth of the section to its left, have them name each section and discuss patterns they see in the names, such as what they notice about the place value names to the left and right of the decimal.

Students create numbers by standing on the chart to determine if a number is greater than, less than, or equal to another. Give each student an index card and have them all write a number between 0 and 9. Starting with numbers to the left of the decimal point, have four students arrange themselves on the chart in the largest whole number possible using their cards. They return to their seats and another group of four students arrange themselves in the smallest number possible. The whole class should write down the numbers that are formed. Students then write on their white-boards or hold up fingers in a horizontal *V* to represent a "greater than" or "less than" sign. You write the correct answer on the board using the appropriate symbols and the comparison of the numbers, such as 4,560 > 1,230.

When students are ready to progress, explain that they will make numbers starting from the tens place and lining up to the right, so they will make a number with a decimal point. The first four students make the largest number they can using the two decimal places, and the next students assemble themselves to represent the smallest possible number following the same placement rule. Again, students write their answers and compare them to the correct answer you write on the board.

For an additional level of challenge, instruct each group to stand to the right of the decimal point, extending the line beyond the hundredths place. Help the class read the new decimal number. Make numbers with more and more places to the right of the decimal, name them, and continue to play the game with students lining up at the designated starting point and forming themselves into the largest and smallest arrangements while the class determines which number is "greater than" another, using the place value chart.

Larger numbers can be done by including more students standing on the number line and making numbers in the billions place as the remaining class members write the number numerically and in word form.

A challenge extension is to ask students if (and why) someone holding a zero in one place on the line has a different value than someone holding a zero in another place on the line. What about zeros after the last number *following* the decimal?

A Matter of Perspective. Change the location of teaching to refresh students' learning perspective. Move to a different side of the room to teach; when you walk around the class, have students turn their heads and torsos to see you. They now have a changed visual background—they see behind you for added input that will alert the RAS.

Alternatively, go outdoors for a math lesson if possible. Use chalk to draw giant graphs of coordinate planes and have students walk to the spot you assign them by giving them the coordinates of the point. Take students on a walk to study from a different point of view. Look for geometric shapes in buildings, nature, sidewalks, and signs. Challenge older students to use their heights and the lengths of their shadows to calculate the height of a tree or flagpole based on its shadow.

Maintaining Motivation

As should be clear by now, motivation is an ongoing concern. Student attention needs to be grabbed from the outset, sustained throughout a lesson, and maintained throughout a unit. To stay motivated, students need *continual* reinforcement. Here are a few more ideas for keeping your students motivated:

- Periodically remind students that their mental effort is relevant to pleasure in the near future. The younger the children, the less tolerant their brains are to activities that are not pleasurable now or expected to be so in the very near future. Fortunately, the dopamine-reward network releases motivating dopamine in *expectation* of pleasure. Let students know which of their enjoyable math activities will be coming up during the lesson and how what they are practicing now connects to the desirable activity. The dopamine release gives you the time you need to work with students on procedures and facts that must be understood for them to build a math foundation, such as multiplication tables or place-value names.
- Periodically ask questions and encourage opinions and predictions related to the big picture, the big question, or the discrepant event that started the lesson to renew students' curiosity. Start with questions that are within all students' achievable-challenge range so they experience the pleasure of success. Ask questions that don't call for a specific answer, such as, "How can you find the sum of . . . ?" or "Who can explain *why* 6 + 7 = 13?" or "What would you do to figure out how many students there are in all three 5th grade classes?"
- Use frequent informal assessment with whiteboards and active participation such as gesture responses that are fun to signify *yes* or *no* (e.g., pat

your head and rub your tummy, spin to the right or left, make a butter-fly or bunny ears with your hands). These activities maintain attention and can help correct misconceptions.

- Purposely make a mistake to see if students are paying attention. As you count aloud by ones or multiples, have students make a thumbs-up when they hear you repeat or skip one (this activity increases listening skills and reduces mistake negativity). Make an obvious mistake during a lesson to see if students are paying attention.

- Use a magic word of the day. Your students are too young to know the Groucho Marx quiz show, but a recurring gag was Groucho's secret word of the day. If one of the contestants said the word in conversation, they would win an extra prize. In some of my lessons, I tell (auditory) and write (visual) the magic word of the day. Instead of saying it to win, the person who first puts a finger on his or her nose when I use the word during class is the winner.

Over time, you'll add to these suggestions with many of your own ideas for motivating students. The results you'll see in terms of attentive students who are eager to learn will, in turn, motivate *you*. It's a win-win situation.

When students come to your class with math negativity, expressed as boredom, disruptive behavior, low effort, or resistance to applying effort, you have the opportunity to change much more than their math success. Because such a high premium is placed on math achievement, students understandably correlate their low performance with their academic abilities in general. If you help them connect to math through their interests, curiosity, and appropriate level of achievable challenge, and if you help them recognize that their efforts to reach achievable goals are bringing them closer to success, then you plant the seeds of hope.

This is when you see the gradual change from the stress of hopelessness and helplessness to the mind-set of the possible. These are the students you successfully set back on paths where they once joyfully counted aloud to all who would listen!

7

Bringing the Real World
to the Math Classroom

It helps me pay attention when teachers put my name in the problem,
"Joaquin has 35 marbles," or when they ask me to tell them what they
just said.

—Joaquin, *7th grade student*

To spur interest in topics, especially challenging ones, start with student-focused, real-world uses of the concept and then gradually progress to the symbolic and abstract representation of the concept. To keep the real-world connections relevant, the "here-me-now" component is critical; without it, the best-constructed plans won't get through the primitive reticular activating system (RAS).

Adding to the suggestions in earlier chapters, this chapter describes ways you can incorporate real-world connections into individual lessons through personal connections aided by "kidwatching" notes; use of real-world tools that rely on mathematics; events that relate to the school, community, or world; and attention to teachable moments. It also includes an example of an activity or project that starts in lower-elementary school and can be extended into later school years. As long-term projects consolidate new learning with existing neural networks, the networks expand, making the foundational and conceptual knowledge available for more real-world transfer applications.

Maximizing Individual Meaning and Personal Relevance

Strong correlations are recognized between people's driving interest in a particular topic and high success (Guthrie & Wigfield, 2000; Palmer, Codling, & Gambrel, 1994). Knowing students' personal interests and a few things that are important to them can enhance instruction by providing the "here-me-now" ingredients needed to get input through the RAS sentry. The following strategies outline various specific ways to use this approach.

♣ STRATEGY: Gather and Use Background Knowledge About Students

Gathering background information about your students is a good way to get what you need to connect them to topics through interest or to incorporate things about them into sample math questions in class. Take clipboard notes during class on random comments students make that include personal information, such as the name of their soccer team or where their grandmother lives. Later, add the information to an index card you keep for each student. Background material can also come from autobiographies that students complete (or that younger students dictate) that include information about their favorite sports, favorite foods, pets, siblings' names, birthdays, favorite TV shows, and so on. You can provide a series of questions to serve as prompts for this autobiographical information. This process is known as "kidwatching."

Once you have these data, use students' names and surprise a student by incorporating the name of his or her dog, brother, favorite food, or favorite soccer team in a sample problem. Students may not be intrinsically interested in long division, but they are interested in each other, so you will motivate listening when the word problem you present includes facts they want to hear about their friends. Consider this example: "Carol went to the market to buy her favorite fruit, bananas, and brought her dog, Frodo. When she got there, she took $5 from the wallet her brother Frank gave her for her birthday . . . ." Even if other students are not interested in the math, they are surprised that you know so much about Carol and are interested in these things about her. They also stay alert for the time you'll use information about them.

You can also acknowledge a student's birthday with calculations already written on the board using his or her name and the numbers in the birth date and year. Write the student's name on the board along with a birthday greeting. Below this, include the student's birth date, for example, 3-12-2001. Depending on the age of your students, a variety of exercises can be done with these numbers, such as organizing them from low to high (or vice versa), adding/subtracting/multiplying/dividing them, ordering the individual digits to create the smallest and largest numbers possible, or calculating how many days came before March 12 in 2001.

You can gain important additional background information from older students by asking them to write "math-experience autobiographies" (using prompt questions), and parents can be invited to include their own insights. These accounts will help you select which strategies to use and avoid, especially when students are having difficulties. These forms are also useful during parent conferences as references, and you can add additional information based on what parents tell you and what you observe in class. You can even include these in portfolios for next year's teachers.

I like to preface this activity by explaining my purpose to students: "As your math teacher, I want to understand your unique view of mathematics, identify your strengths and weaknesses, and help you have the best possible experience in math this year." I then use the following questions to elicit responses that help guide my instruction. The responses included below each prompt are examples of actual student responses I have received over the years. You can see how these responses provide valuable insight into individual students' strengths, weaknesses, likes, and dislikes.

What have your experiences in math classes been like?
- not challenging enough
- challenging, but not impossible
- perfect for my skill level

Which topics in math have been especially difficult for you?
- fractions—especially adding fractions with different denominators
- converting decimals to fractions and percents
- negative numbers
- area and perimeter

How do you feel about math in general?
- Math overwhelms me.
- I really enjoy working with numbers—they seem to click in my mind.
- Math was my least favorite subject, but you make it fun so I can pay attention.

What do you like about group work?
- It is social.
- It is easier to ask a friend a question you might not ask in class.
- Groups are helpful because I have someone else's point of view.

What do you do when you get "stuck"?
- I move on to the next problem and come back to the problem later.
- I read the problem over more carefully.
- I check the book to study the examples.

Describe some of your best study habits.
- take good notes, check my notes
- draw diagrams
- do problems from each section before a test
- make mnemonic devices
- make a picture of it in my mind

How do you memorize something you have to memorize?
- repeat it in my mind
- sing it to a tune
- say it aloud
- review it three times and then again

What did you do differently when you were most successful compared to when you were less successful?
- I kept calm.
- I listened more and didn't space out.
- I checked my work.
- I started reading the directions before jumping into the problem.
- I brought my materials to class each day.

What did past teachers do that helped you learn most?
- They let us choose how we wanted to learn.
- They had fun with math—it is contagious.
- They were patient.
- They relate the problems to something interesting.
- My best teacher really knew how my mind works.

What problems did you have with some math teachers in the past?
- They get frustrated easily.
- Stern teachers are unhelpful; relaxed teachers help me learn.
- When they are not nice I lose focus.
- When I asked for help he said, "What's not to get?"

In what ways have you used math outside of school?
- counting money
- figuring out cost of things on sale
- calculate my batting average
- geometry to make plays in soccer

Do your parents or other close relatives or adult family friends use math in their jobs or hobbies? What are those jobs or hobbies where they use math?
- organizing their business
- measuring wood
- accountant
- banker
- selling cars and calculating what to charge to make a profit

♣ STRATEGY: Make Personal Connections with Homework or Class Work

There are an endless number of ways to help students make personal connections with homework or class work. Younger students can make bar graphs that show the frequency of each letter in their first and last names. Partners can create Venn diagrams comparing and contrasting their favorite sports. Older students can solve mean/mode/median problems using data from their favorite sports team's scores.

You can use information about all or most students to make them more attentive to questions: "Our math textbook was written in 1999. Most of you were born in 2002 or 2003. How many years before you were born was your book published?" "Our school scored in the top 20 percent in recycling. There were 80 schools in the evaluation. How many schools did we beat because you are so good at recycling?"

When you tell students how a math topic connects to *your* own interests, your enthusiasm will influence their own opinions. The amygdala picks up on facial and verbal expressions of happiness and responds with open channels to the prefrontal cortex (Wang, Rao, & Wetmoree, 2005). Seeing your excitement, students will react with more interest.

Connect to Mathematicians. Before introducing a math formula or procedure that is attributed to a particular mathematician, look on the Internet for biographical information about that person, such as an interesting anecdote or a significant event in his or her life that took place when the person was the same age as the students in your class. Start class by telling the information as a story about someone, as if the person were alive today and this event took place when he or she was the same age as your students. Students will see the relevant math as a creation of a real person, just like themselves, and relating to the person makes it easier to relate to the math.

Ask older students to think about what theories, formulas, and technologies were in place that may have given the mathematician the background to develop the procedure or theorem they are learning. Discuss challenges or setbacks that occurred during the course of the mathematician's work so your students realize that math was a struggle even for the most brilliant math superstars.

Allow Students to Make the Connection. It is important for students to value the information we need to teach them, so we should make those links clear to them. You can sometimes let students make their own connections (save their ideas to use in the future) by asking them, "How will knowing this help you now or in the future?"

Many students, Explorers in particular, like getting information from the Internet or using computer technology to create a Web page or an attractive document with images. These students are motivated, and retain information more successfully, when they can use computers to present math information. Be sure to share the products of their work with the rest of the class, grade, and school, if possible.

STRATEGY: Find Teachable Moments in Math

A student in my math class learning about positive and negative correlations asked when this knowledge would be useful in "real life." I asked his classmates for suggestions, and they provided a number of examples, such as comparing the amount of money earned by different professionals and years of schooling, or comparing the weight of a car and its gas mileage. After a few minutes, another student asked how the graphs we were using would help her in a future job. I asked her what job she had in mind, and she said working at a retail clothes store. I explained that if her goal was to be a clerk or cashier, she would probably have no use for the knowledge. However, if she wanted to be a manager, she might want to find which factors in potential employees correlate with the successful fit of an applicant in a job. For example, she could keep records on different variables among employees—such as age, race, hair color, years of school, and gender—to see if any of those variables had a positive correlation with the number of sales made by those employees.

I knew that I had included some controversial variables, and I wanted to see if students would respond. To my delight, they did. A lively discussion ensued about the legality and ethics of both looking for links between gender or race and sales success and whether such data should be considered by corporate management in making hiring decisions. I knew we were off topic and wouldn't finish the day's math lesson, but the value of these students having this discussion (and, indeed, it was student-centered, as they bounced their ideas and concerns among each other with minimal input from me) was more important than the day's math. These students were considering topics that they could someday actually confront in their future jobs.

✤ STRATEGY: Relate Negative Integers to Real Life

Brainstorm together (or give small groups different tools for this purpose) to discover how negative integers are related to real life. To start, instead of making a link to the words *negative integers* in examples you present, use phrases such as "less than zero," and when students use the word *negative,* reinforce it by repeating their words. However, don't explain the meaning of *negative* at this point. The idea is for students to develop the concept before giving it a label, especially one with possible "negative" memories such as previous difficulty with the topic. The following are some examples that students may suggest or that you could give to small groups.

Outside Temperatures. Place a thermometer outside a window so students can make daily calculations and keep a chart reporting the actual temperature and the temperature change from the previous day. Students will see that the change can be a negative number without the temperature falling below 0—an often-confusing concept that is clarified by these observations.

An achievable-challenge extension could include barometers, and students who need more advanced work can learn how negative—or falling—barometric pressure can predict rain. Students' intrinsic pleasure in using mathematics to make correct weather predictions adds positive emotional context to the memory and increases its durability.

Water and Ice. Have students use glasses of water and ice cubes in a container to track temperature changes. They can record and evaluate the relationship between the number of ice cubes added and change in temperature. Later, the cubes can represent the concept of adding negative numbers—"adding coldness."

A more abstract progression from here is for students to visualize what happens when they leave the freezer door open. Are they adding or taking away coldness? They can then think of subtracting (taking away) a negative integer as taking away coldness so the temperature, or number on the number line, goes up and becomes more positive (warmer) when coldness is taken away.

Ocean Views. A picture of the ocean that includes above- and underwater views can help students visualize changes in depth. This activity is more fun if each group has a little plastic diver or one cut out from a magazine or a picture of a diver pulled from the Internet. Ask questions such as,

"If you are the diver at 5 feet below sea level and drop down another 4 feet, where are you?" This questioning would advance to higher levels, such as, "What is the change in feet the diver makes as he goes from 2 feet below the surface to 8 feet below?" Then, to demonstrate that positive numbers can be the answer when still working on the negative number line, ask, "What is the change in feet the diver makes as he goes from 10 feet below the surface to 4 feet below?"

Students ready for higher challenge can create problems for each other that are more complex, such as figuring out where the diver is after two changes in depth. They can also be "consultants" to other groups.

Envelopes and IOUs. Present an example such as this: "I borrow $5 from you one day, and the next day I pay you back $3, so now my debt is $2." Students can have envelopes where they place IOUs that change each day as you tell them what happens to their finances: "Yesterday your IOU said that I owed you $2, but today you borrow $3 for the bake sale. Write a new IOU for *your* debt to me." Students doing advanced work can use copies of checking account registers with more complex and multiple transactions.

Incorporating Real-World Math from Students' Daily Lives

Just as personal relevance and connections to students' interests both promote attention with "here-me-now" impact, giving students a goal that they consider worthy of their effort helps students identify what they want to know and recognize what you have to teach. For example, learning area and perimeter are more valuable when students see sample blueprints they will create and know that, once their plans are approved by the "city building commission" (where the calculations must be right to get a permit), they will construct their buildings in class with cardboard.

♣ STRATEGY: Use Math to Make a Home

To students, there is nothing as "real" as their homes and neighborhoods, and from kindergarten on, the math concepts of measurement, ratio, proportion, estimation, prediction, and trial-error-correct can all be motivated by the "here-me-now" of where students live. For each of these real-world connections to math concept applications, you'll find that many students will be even more engaged when their measurements are used to make models of their homes or maps of their neighborhoods.

This activity is one that can begin in the lower grades—even kindergarten—and continue through later years. Sketches of a young student's room that focus on relative size and positioning of objects can begin with simple measurements and progress over the years to more complex measurements, including area and volume. The extensions from year to year follow the same skill applications that students use for their own rooms, but they can progress to designing (or constructing) their house, town, or even a fictional/dream house or town. Two-dimensional measurements progress to three dimensions, and students can ultimately incorporate the models, calculations, trigonometry, and graphing of three-dimensional space.

This activity serves as a motivator to both brain filters and the dopamine-reward system because it includes choices, creativity, and opportunities to use learning strengths and favored strategies for success. Explorer learners often let their imaginations lead them, and the calculations and plans follow. Map Reader learners enjoy the sequential planning and organization using their favored strategies such as time lines, graphic organizers, and step-by-step detailed plans that involve calculations first, followed by drawing or construction. Additional motivators can include a photo album or portfolio of their work on these maps and models through the years. The portfolio is also something that can be used for assessment, demonstrating levels of mastery and conceptual knowledge to future teachers.

Depending on the grade, each version of this activity can be adapted to core math concepts that are extended each year so prior knowledge is reactivated and concept circuits are extended. Each core topic is planned as a progression in accord with the K–12 standards, but each year the students know they have some background knowledge and experience that started in kindergarten. The confidence of having completed those earlier projects and the visual evidence of the progress they make maintain students' motivation and perseverance through challenge and errors to go to the next step. Core math concepts that can be the focus of these activities include measurement, geometric shapes and characteristics, ratio, proportion, and graphing.

Executive functions also grow, as the activities increasingly require judgment, goal setting, organization, prediction, critical thinking, data analysis, decision making, cooperation, communication, and metacognition.

From early geometry (identifying basic shapes in the classroom) through the development of core geometric concepts, students learn to incorporate specific angles (acute and right angles); three-, four-, and five-sided polygons; and parallel and perpendicular lines in their designs. Throughout this process, students also progress from data gathered by simple observation and estimation (such as measuring lengths of furniture with lines of their shoes) to more precise measurements using technology and Internet resources such as aerial views of their neighborhood.

Fundamental calculations and procedures also advance through the grades. For example, students can calculate the cost of bricks or wood (to construct a dream house) in a lower grade, and eventually calculate the costs of labor, materials, and construction time. In upper grades, students can be given actual construction rules to follow, and they can create spreadsheets to present to classmates who form the architectural/construction/land-use-permit-approval committee. Web sites such as MapQuest and Google Maps can be used as resources for distance calculations in their own town, and Google Earth provides map information that can be manipulated to vary size perspectives for additional questions, such as determining where new buildings should be placed based on different parameters, including open space, proximity to schools, and geographic considerations that add construction costs to a potential project.

Throughout this highly adaptable project, students benefit from continuity across grades, and they recognize the benefit of more precise mathematical calculation tools and the executive functions of planning and prioritizing. They sustain motivation because each year they recognize an increase in the accuracy and competence they acquire as their math skills reflect their progress on a real-world activity that has true personal meaning to them.

✤ STRATEGY: Bring in Real-World Experience

In addition to motivating the "here-me-now" processing in students' brains, real-world connections can incorporate creative problem solving, communication, collaboration, and critical analysis. After students finish an activity, encourage them to describe what they liked about it. When their comments relate to any of these important 21st-century skills, link their words to the more formal terms for higher-level thinking they used. For example, explain the meaning of "judgment" and "analysis" for younger children, and ask for examples of each from older students. Using the function name extends motivation as students sense the adultlike qualities they are using when they "prioritize," for example. The result is increased math positivity and self-confidence as students are made aware of the value of the skills they achieve.

Class visitors can show or tell your students how the math concepts your class is *currently studying* are used for parts of jobs that students would consider fun and interesting. Individualized motivation opportunities include pairing students who show high interest in these presentations with the relevant professional for mentoring or part of a day "on the job." This is an especially good alternative for some students who might not otherwise be able to participate in the national Take Your Child to Work Day.

As you go about your errands or visit professionals or technical specialists for your personal needs, continue to keep your students in mind. Even if there doesn't seem to be a good match for the current year's students, ask if the professional might consider doing a presentation or having a student shadow him or her in the future. Keep a list of these people, as well as a list of current and previous students' parents who express a willingness to do a presentation or have an occasional student shadow (consider adding this option, if it is not already part of the paperwork, to the information cards that parents fill out on Back to School Night). Once you start keeping your list, you'll realize that bakers, chefs, local retail business owners, auto mechanics, computer repair professionals, interior decorators, architects, and party planners are all potential real-world motivators for your students. They are motivators who can show *how* they use the very math skills your students are learning, and they can connect those skills with students' interests.

After such real-world exposure, my students have reported on the specific math problems they worked on with their mentors. The positive response to these reports from even my most reluctant math students reminds me that the opinions of students' friends are priceless and often have more influence than anything I can tell them about the value of math.

✤ STRATEGY: Create a Room Chart for Student Contributions

It is helpful for students to think about where they saw math or how they may have used it outside the classroom. Students can cut out newspaper ads, bring in menus, or write about the math they used when they built a birdhouse or found the best price on an item offered with different discounts and rebates.

I also welcome examples of graphs or statistics found in newspaper ads that give false impressions, such as one showing only the very top of bar graphs to magnify what is really a small difference between several companies' products. Other items for this chart could include batting averages, interest rates on savings accounts, and historical references in movies or novels relative to math (such as the price of particular items in the 1800s, which students can compare to current prices).

Encourage your students to share things that have to do with math and numbers that they notice as they go on trips or shopping. Let them hear you use math to solve problems, such as how you calculated whether you had enough money for popcorn at the movies when you needed to keep two dollars to pay for parking. Remind students that errands with their parents to an office supply store or hardware store are opportunities to explore tools of measurement and compare large volumes to small volumes for *more than* and *less than,* percents, discounts, and sales tax. Offer "extra credit" for contributions to the bulletin board or for reporting on the use of math outside the classroom.

✤ STRATEGY: Use Students' Likes and Dislikes

Few things motivate as much as a common goal—either to get something everyone wants or to change or abolish something that everyone doesn't like. Keep the question narrow enough so students' answers aren't all about not liking tests and homework, and you will come up with shared complaints, such as long cafeteria lines, slow traffic lights on the way to school, too little time between classes, or deceptive advertising that makes it appear as if a specific brand of cereal contains more marshmallows than it actually does.

Keep a list of these "I'm mad" statements on the board and include a second column of ideas titled "What I can do about it." When engaged in a math unit, see which class concern can be evaluated mathematically, and ask students what they would like the situation to change into. In other words, what is the ideal situation that would make the problem go away? Once students are all motivated by a common goal, introduce the mathematical "solution."

If students want to protest to the principal about a long lunch line, what information do they need to prove their point, and what solutions can they offer? If you want to teach calculating the mean (averaging), listen for ideas that can be evaluated by knowing how to do those calculations. When students offer investigative suggestions, such as finding out how long the wait is on different days and figuring out why it is longer on some days than others, you have your opportunity to guide them so they *want to know what you have to teach.*

It will soon become evident that students need data to see if there is a pattern. After they suggest, for example, timing the wait for each student in line during different parts of the lunch hour and taking those measurements for a week, then what? Can they just give the principal all those numbers as they are? What will that prove? Students will realize that something must be done to summarize their data so the information is powerful and proves something. Once students discover trends, they can write a real report to the principal stating, for example, that the average wait in the lunch line between 12:10 and 12:30 on sloppy joe days is 10 minutes, but when the lunch is mac and cheese, the mean is only 6 minutes.

Just as novel music related to a lesson won't automatically pop into your head each time you plan a lesson, neither will students' potential likes or dislikes. However, as you listen attentively, you'll develop a new awareness of songs, events, news items, and other things in which students might have an interest.

As with "kidwatching," jot down the names of songs that could fit with future lessons, or take note of potential issues that might interest students, such as the long line of cars that forms to drop off students on rainy days. Encourage students to tell you when they hear a good math-related song or have a gripe. As your list of possible investigations grows and you see the list every day, your own brain will make the links, and you'll have an "aha!" moment when you realize that the rainy day car problem can be a great motivator for number lines or graphing as students evaluate alternative drop-off points around the school perimeter.

Using "Found Math" Ideas

Opportunities to motivate math engagement with high-interest, "here-me-now" activities are all around you. For example, once you realize that certain dates are special—such as the fact that September 10, 2011, just after 6 a.m. could be written as 06:07:08 09/10/11—you will be attuned to make notes and gather lots of real-*student*-world math options to introduce. Keep this pad of ideas nearby when planning lessons, and you'll be impressed by how frequently great ideas will pop out at you. Here are some to start you off.

♣ STRATEGY: Use Mail-Order Catalogs

Younger students can use catalogs to find the largest number of items they can buy with $100 or the largest number of items in their favorite color that they can buy, coming as close to $100 as possible without going over. Alternatively, how long will it take them to save up for the item they want most if they earn $2 a week, or, for older children, $2 an hour when they mow lawns and $3 an hour when they babysit or shovel snow? What are the different ways they can do both jobs and earn the amount they need?

You'll find ideas that students can use from these catalogs in the questions you choose from their math textbooks. For older students, depending on the topic, you can have them calculate percent sales tax while answering the same questions. When students consider purchases with real catalogs offering things they like, they are more motivated and able to see the value of math in their lives.

♣ STRATEGY: Work It Out

What could be more "here-me-now" than students' own heartbeats? You can have students measure their pulse, run in place for a set number of seconds, and then check their pulse again for various comparisons and class averages. Extensions include determining the rate per second after they stop running and how long it takes until their pulse returns to their original resting level. (This measurement is actually the calculation most correlated with fitness and can be discussed to promote exercise. Students can be encouraged to evaluate their success with aerobic exercise training by keeping records of this pulse recovery time.)

♣ STRATEGY: Use Big Events and Holidays

"Big events" include activities at school such as a jog-a-thon, a school carnival, an academic decathlon, math competitions, and sporting events (local, national, international) that have lots of numbers and opportunities for calculations. When I carried the 2002 Olympic relay torch and my students ran along the road beside me, they wanted to know all about the torch. As they passed it around, I explained my torch-carrying instructions: "You are supposed to hold it straight out, so even though it only weighs about four pounds it will seem quite heavy during your quarter-mile run, so feel free to switch hands."

The students felt the weight for themselves and wanted to know why the situation described would be true. The event provided a perfect time to review or preview graphing, to make intake-output tables, or to do algebra equations using the variables of distance with the constant of weight. You don't need an Olympic torch to do this activity, of course. Students can experience this phenomenon by holding a large can of soup out at different distances. Then they can experiment with a scale with a fulcrum and sliding trays as they try to balance different weights by moving the fulcrum point. (This recognition that weight can stay constant but force can increase based on distance from a fulcrum is one of the measures of children's numeracy level.)

Be a Musher. The students in my 5th grade class had been assigned summer reading about a girl musher in the Iditarod race. I knew their prior knowledge would be motivating, so when the date of the actual race approached, I went to the official Web site to find the names and numbers of the year's mushers. I planned my own activities and found more on the Web site in their "For Teachers" section, including interactive tracking and a link to "Pick a Math Standard: Design a Lesson." I had each student select from a jar the names of two mushers from the original field of about 80, which left more in the jar for children whose musher dropped out early.

Our activities began with simple calculations, such as the number of booties based on the 16 dogs a musher started with, and extended to measurements of the trail; metric conversion; graphing distance and time for the concept of rate; temperature changes for adding, subtracting, bar graphs, or negative integers; and even geometry, for finding shapes on the sled and using the Pythagorean theorem to calculate the flight distance from musher location to the nearest veterinary hospital. Even mean, median, mode, and range become valuable "here-me-now" concepts when they relate to the temperatures on the course and the distances between students' assigned mushers.

I used "musher math" to do a series of activities to review the year's lessons just in time for the state test. March (the date of the Iditarod) is sometimes a touchy month, leading up to spring break and testing, so the timing of this race and the many associated activities is perfect. When calculations are based on the musher's position along the race course, students work at their level of achievable challenge with different levels of calculations. Students gather comparison data using information about "their" mushers, such as comparing how long it would take their musher to catch up to the lead musher if he or she sped up by 2 miles per hour (and then, to add more complexity, if the lead musher sped up by 1 mile an hour at the same time).

Each afternoon when I posted the rankings, students came back from lunch recess early to see how "they" were doing. It took no prompting for them to get out their pencils and calculate how far their musher had gone in the past day and how much farther he or she had to go to get to the next stop or to the finish line in Nome. You know you are doing something right when students come in early to do math!

Honor the Presidents. Money motivates. Prior to Presidents' Day Weekend, hang a $1 bill and a $5 bill (very high up) in your classroom. As students get excited, ask questions such as these: "Which presidents are honored this weekend?" "Are there any hints on the bills?" Then you can move to all kinds of number activities, such as working with partners to see how many calculations they can make using the numerals 1 and 5. For older students, remind them that they can use exponents, fractions, or other procedures. For more combinations and to add history knowledge to the lesson, incorporate or change the numbers to 1 and 16 and see if students know why you selected those numbers.

You'll find that students are motivated simply by seeing the $1 and $5 bills in the classroom, even though they know the money is not for them. Money motivates even when it is not real because it is associated with pleasure, and that means RAS attention and dopamine release.

Make Time Fly. When the seasonal time changes occur, moving clocks ahead or back an hour, the school clock and some students' watches have often not been reset. You might start the lesson by asking if anyone was early or late to something on Sunday because they forgot about the time change. Interest is heightened with this introduction, so in lower grades plan one of your "telling time" lessons for these days. In upper grades, use whatever procedure you are teaching to do calculations based on different time zones (this even works for negative integers and time lines). You can print a time zone map from the Internet and have students pick countries that they'd like to visit or that have personal relevance and do level-appropriate calculations about time differences.

Taking Advantage of Real-World Multimedia Applications

Textbook examples work well as templates when creating meaningful problems connected to your students' interests, school activities, "kidwatching" cards, and current events, and many are available online to match with the current unit and associated standards. However, you can go even further with computer-based programs and fun games designed for foundational-skill practice but enhanced with the creative expertise of programmers who know what children of different ages enjoy playing. With the added bonuses of alignment with standards and progress-monitoring results available for teachers, computer experiences in math are ideal for learning, practice, and development of the technical literacy that our students need for 21st-century careers and interests.

♣ STRATEGY: Use Computer Simulations

It is no surprise that excellent computer simulations are available for mathematics that offer appropriate challenge, multisensory options tied to learning strengths, choice, corrective feedback, and records of student progress for teacher evaluation. In the Internet Resources section (Appendix A), I've listed the programs that I've used successfully with my students, but programs change and are dropped from the Internet, so you'll need to evaluate them on your own before allowing students to use them.

One of the favorites designed for upper-elementary school (from the Web site www.coolmath-games.com), is Lemonade Stand. The goal of this game is to make as much profit as possible within 30 days as the operator of a lemonade stand. Students control pricing, inventory, purchasing of supplies, and quality (they discover that too much ice is costly and dilutes flavor, but not enough ice is problematic on a warm day—hence the value of checking the weather prediction option that the game offers). The game is so much fun that my middle school students (who cannot select it during class time as it is too basic to add to their conceptual or procedural knowledge) come in during lunch and recess to play with math!

There are many free real-world simulations for multiple grade levels and topics on the Cool Math Games site. Once you evaluate them, you'll be able to add them to your chart of real-world links for your yearlong lesson plan.

Compelling games for teenagers are more difficult to recommend. The math games that appeal to teenagers usually involve violence or gore, but some are so well designed for conceptual and multifactor analysis that I recommend taking a look at them and deciding if they will work for your students.

One of the most popular games is Dimenxian (http://dimenxian.en. softonic.com). It begins with a bio-digital virus released on a remote island that threatens to infect the world's ecosystem and destroy mankind. Mathematics is required (linear equation analysis, graphing, and application) to disengage the virus, restore the island to its original environment, and defend against mutations. This is a pre-algebra or early algebra program. Though programmed with points for teamwork, it can be modified for advanced independent work as it does follow the achievable-challenge model.

Games like this that apply procedures to new situations are of interest to students and use mental manipulation in the transfer of learning (Din & Calao, 2001). This game is worth trying yourself as a good example of what to look for in math simulation games. It is multisensory and engaging in graphics and interaction; it offers feedback with opportunities to find alternative ways to solve problems; and it enables the player to correct errors with modifications to the appropriate procedure. In addition, it is a useful assessment tool because students' actions are not only recorded but also analyzed to reveal patterns of errors that indicate which topics advanced students need to participate in when teaching specific topics to the whole class. You can then assign homework practice in the revealed areas of weakness.

✤ STRATEGY: Use Stock Market Math

Another activity that students enjoy can be found at www.stockmarket game.org. My students actually remind me to let them use it because they know that it links to my curriculum plan for the year. I allow them to see my plans for the year because I like students to see that I plan and organize using both short- and long-term goals. This sharing is a form of modeling that benefits their own development of this executive function.

Stock Market Math is another standards-based program, but it is above the level of most students until 3rd or 4th grade. It can be an excellent independent activity for students to work on when they have mastered the current topic. Because you can link the advanced levels of the concept in the program to the concepts that the rest of the class is working on, students using Stock Market Math can share their discoveries or experiences with classmates as a way to work on their communication skills and to motivate classmates who see what they will be able to do with a bit more foundational knowledge.

The basic program offers opportunities to transfer grade level–specific math learning and concepts to economic fundamentals using students' "brokerage accounts." Although it is set up for small groups to use, as teams build the prefrontal cortex functions of negotiation and cooperation, it can be modified if you have only one or two students ready to work at this level. Both individual activity and team participation incorporate critical analysis and decision making and develop technological literacy while students learn the importance of saving money and the risks and benefits of investing—information that is sadly lacking from most schools and even colleges.

Schools pay about $17 a team for the full Stock Market Math curriculum, which includes access to a computer system that executes simulated trades and ranks teams by states and age group. At the end of the term, the teams with the best returns in each state take home bull and bear trophies, gift certificates, or other prizes.

♣ STRATEGY: Play Math Games with Patterning

Children enjoy games that allow them to make guesses and improve accuracy. This kind of activity also exercises the brain's patterning skills, which is critical to extending concepts by consolidating new input with prior knowledge. Students also develop positive associations with memorized arithmetic when they practice with reinforcing games and activities. These can be workstation or center activities, small-group activities that take place while you work with students on more direct instruction, or celebrations for successful completion of units.

Board or manipulative games for math skills and concepts include Battleship, checkers, chess, Connect Four, dominoes, Mastermind, Othello, Pente, concentration card or board games, Jenga, Monopoly, 3-D tic-tac-toe, Rummikub, and tangrams. These are all great games for teaching logical thinking and practicing mathematical reasoning. Card games such as go fish, crazy eights, rummy, solitaire, hearts, and war also involve mathematical reasoning. The war card game can be used for an addition or multiplication game. The dealer passes out all the cards, but players don't look at their cards. Each player turns up two cards. In addition war, the highest sum wins the hand. In multiplication war, the highest product wins the hand. Play continues until one player has no more cards. These games engage mathematical neural circuits, as do sudoku and math puzzles. Learning or trying to figure out card tricks also gets the neuron circuits buzzing.

Poker has also been recommended for older students because it involves prediction and patterning, as players need to not only evaluate their own hands but also deduce their opponents' cards. Chess can help students develop critical-thinking skills, such as prediction and analysis. Students who become familiar with the vertical and horizontal lines of a chess board—and how they are numbered—also learn the fundamentals of map and graph coordinates.

✤ STRATEGY: Play Scaffolding Games for Differentiated Levels

Deal or No Deal. Players take turns rolling two dice and keep a running sum of total points (depending on age and ability, this can be done mentally for mental math practice or scaffolded with pencil and paper for computation practice). The goal is to score as many points as possible without going over 100. Students must roll both dice each time. Players alternate who goes first, but the game point goes to the player who comes closest to 100 without going over.

Team Games. Jeopardy can be played by dividing the class into two teams. If a player gets an answer correct, his or her team gets two points. If the player asks for help from teammates and says the correct answer, his or her team gets one point. Errors get no points and no penalty. The game can be easily adapted for any grade, using anything from multiplication facts to negative-integer multiplication. Students can ask you for "hot," "very hot," or "super hot" questions and win points accordingly.

Students can help you prepare questions to use for the game while they work in homogeneous achievable-challenge groups for the given topic. In their groups, they create questions for the levels you assign them, with the most advanced group writing "super hot" questions. After students in these groups write individual questions, they pass them around to be sure they all get the same answer, and if not, they should work together to figure out which is correct. If there are enough students to form two groups each for each level of questions, these groups should be on opposing teams so they won't be answering their own questions during the game. If there are not enough students at the level, just change one part of the question when you use it. Code the question cards in advance for level of difficulty. Added support can be provided by allowing responders to consult with "lifeline" team members before giving a final answer.

Math Bingo. Have students fill out bingo cards with the numbers 1 through 25, in any order they choose (use fewer boxes for younger students). Roll three dice and write the three numbers on the board. In teams or individually, students use the three individual numbers with any math procedure to try to get a column, row, or diagonal filled in on their bingo cards. The rules are that students must use all three numbers in each calculation and cannot use any of the three numbers more than once per calculation. Options for older students include the use of square roots, exponents, and parentheses. Allow students who need scaffolding to use individual numbers alone or just two numbers instead of three. When a majority of students want a new set of numbers, throw the dice again. Students cannot mix and match numbers from different throws.

To keep students engaged, and to increase opportunities for success and fun, students can rotate partners in a regular pattern. Partners work together, but be sure that both are involved in the thinking and learning process. Establish the rule that you can, at any time, ask either partner how they used the die values to calculate a bingo number. In other words, they are both required to be able to explain what they did.

Hot Potato. Teams of four to six students sit in a circle and pass a piece of paper on a clipboard with a pen attached. After a lesson, or as a test review, a topic is announced and students write something they recall about the topic (or a sample calculation) on the clipboard when it is passed to them. A sample topic might be cue words that mean addition (or subtraction, multiplication, division, etc.). The clipboards are passed around for one to two minutes, depending on students' age and the number of students in the group.

If a student cannot think of something to add, he or she can ask the group for help, but the student must write the words or numbers independently. This gives the student the review experience and the written reminder. Because the student wrote the answer, he or she still feels a sense of participation and accomplishment.

At the end of the specified time, the team with the most correct data points *not also written by any other team* wins. By not counting items that are contained on multiple lists, the reading of answers adds to the review because students are motivated to listen to opponents' answers and calculate their scores. Representatives from each team take turns reading out their data and skipping the ones that other teams have already said until all items are reported. Any class member may challenge the accuracy of a fact, but you are the final judge.

This chapter introduced a variety of strategies and activities that are based on recognizable "real-world" situations. These familiar contexts provide wonderful opportunities to motivate math learning that are based on students' "here-me-now" perspectives of what is important enough in their own lives to be worthy of mathematics effort. As you try these strategies, you'll find that planning and preparation are not too complex and, when you add a few each year, that your own skills at developing motivating (and meaningful) lessons will likewise increase.

8

Creating Student Goals
for Motivation

....

Obstacles are those frightful things you see when you take your eyes off
your goal.

—Henry Ford

The ability to maintain motivation toward long-term goals, persevere
through challenges, and avoid immediate gratification is not part of a hard-
wired network in the brain of most students until they are in their 20s. As
an executive function that is directed by the prefrontal cortex, long-term,
goal-directed behaviors need to be prompted and promoted in students,
rather than left to chance or "expected of them."

Knowing what motivates the brain to reflect instead of react to the
temptations of immediate gratification in pursuit of long-term goals can
guide instruction for short-term attentive learning and help students experience the intrinsic rewards available when both short- and long-term goals
are met. Instruction that connects with students' interests, is consistent
with their achievable-challenge levels, offers opportunities for choice, rec-
ognizes short-term progress toward a larger goal, delivers helpful feedback, and increases student optimism has the most significant impact on
student motivation and perseverance.

In this chapter, the motivators to achieve established goals—such as
choice, interest, and effort—are related to practical strategic interventions that guide students in the development of appropriate behaviors and
mind-sets.

Motivating for Unit Goals and Core Concepts

Something as simple as the creation of a KWL chart (described in Chapter 3) at the beginning of a unit increases student ownership because students ask questions and identify aspects of a subject about which they are curious. They develop goals about what they want to learn, and when students see that they (individually or as a class) already know a good deal of information related to the new topic, stress goes down and optimism goes up. The following strategies provide other ideas that motivate students to develop meaningful goals for learning.

✤ STRATEGY: Gain Student Interest from the Beginning

When previewing topics you'll cover in a unit, rather than naming processes such as *mixed numbers* or *improper fractions,* use sample problems that demonstrate the usefulness of the procedure, using the personalization strategies suggested earlier. Incorporate information about how the new topic relates to what students have recently studied in other subjects and how it relates to previously mastered concepts. Start the unit with global connections to students' lives through discussion; demonstration; surprising, curiosity-arousing videos, photographs, or facts; or humor related to the topic.

Start by "selling" the parts of the unit that you know will be particularly engaging. For example, as part of a unit on percentages, use a simulation of personal banking to introduce the concept of using percentage to calculate interest. Give students blank checks, a check register, and deposit slips, then create ability-level tiers of transactions for them to use the "money" in their accounts. Students can "save" to purchase items for which they know the cost, or select items from a shopping catalog you have in class. Every day or so, have students make "deposits" to their accounts and update the class balance.

Have students make "deposits" of the same amount of money to their accounts (all students also start with the same amount). Younger students will not be ready to use percentages or calculate interest, but they will be able to subtract whole numbers (rounding off prices if possible) for their purchases. Remind students that they must be able to afford their purchases. In other words, they must have the required amount of money in their accounts to make a purchase—there is no credit. Help young students become familiar with the concepts of *principal* and *interest.*

Advanced options for each unit can be introduced gradually so students aren't overwhelmed. Some should be offered at the beginning, so students who have negative attitudes because of boredom will have something that motivates them from the start. For example, students can calculate interest by having their checking accounts be interest-bearing checking accounts.

In the case of percentage and interest, students can use the Internet or newspapers to compare several banks' interest rates and determine which is the best. Extend the math to economics and have students take notes to share later about the differences, advantages, and disadvantages of various banks' plans and policies. Under what circumstances would they *personally choose* one over another?

When a lesson or block of lessons is full of facts to memorize, consider how you can help your students look forward to appealing activities that will be part of the unit. For example, for standard-to-metric conversions, explain that one homework assignment will be to "translate" a recipe from a cookbook, and the class will vote on the recipe they would like to prepare in class.

Another way to motivate students at the start of a unit is to tell them they'll be teaching a lesson to students in a lower grade. Knowing in advance that they will teach a math concept to "buddies" who are a few grades behind them motivates students to put more effort into learning a concept fully and keeps their minds focused when they practice. You can encourage them to follow your model and seek ways that the procedure or concept relates to their world and that of the younger student. Higher achievable challenge can offer students the opportunity to select a more advanced example of an application of the unit concept and demonstrate or teach part of it to the class (or to you if they are uncomfortable showing their mastery to others).

✤ STRATEGY: Develop Personalized Goals

After communicating learning goals of the new unit to your students, help them make connections between these goals and their personal goals. When students develop personal mastery goals, they will relate what they consider worthy to the unit goals, approach the unit with more focus, and have the dopamine-pleasure response from positive expectation.

Although the brain filters give preferential admittance to "here-me-now" threat- or pleasure-promising sensory input, children can develop pleasure from intrinsic satisfaction, such as reaching meaningful goals. Initially, these goals need to be short-term, but with the right support and achievable challenge, students can extend their tolerance for delaying immediate gratification to achieve that intrinsic satisfaction.

As students' interests, strengths, and talents are used to build up their abilities to focus and persevere at required academic tasks, they build self-confidence from their successes. This increased sense of their own competence helps them persevere when obstacles arise. With each success, they develop their abilities to set and achieve higher goals for themselves, while also building patience, resilience, and greater tolerance for occasional setbacks.

An example of how this process can be used in the classroom comes from a talented ballet dancer in one of my 7th grade advanced algebra classes. This girl was a gifted math student in problem solving, concepts, and number manipulation, but she was uncomfortable with the technology in graphing calculators. She was able to do well in 7th grade using her mathematical skills, but eventually she was going to need to use a graphing calculator for advanced math classes.

To increase her comfort and interest in working with a graphing calculator, I connected the calculator to a CRV ranger—a handheld device used to measure the speed and distance of moving objects, similar to a highway patrol officer's speed gun. I showed her how the system could be used to record a graph of simple dance steps. With her interest stimulated, she delighted in learning what she needed to operate the graphing system. Once her original reluctance was eliminated by personal interest and success, she became comfortable learning the other skills needed for proficiency in using the graphing calculator.

Because immediate pleasure is still what directs your students' focus, short-term goals with pleasurable outcomes are the way to begin. Consider ways to celebrate whole-class goal achievement as well as individual achievable-challenge goals; for example, successful students can be the supply monitor that day, or you can have them decorate a small name card and place it on a class bulletin board titled "Today I reached my goal!"

✤ STRATEGY: Use the Motivating Power of Choice

Adding choice helps diminish the feeling of powerlessness that students develop as a result of their math negativity and gives them a sense of ownership of their learning goals. There is emotional value in the initial sense of empowerment that students experience when they know that they will have some choice in *how* they approach a unit of study, even though they may not be able to choose what to study and when. Even limited choice can make a great difference in students' ultimate engagement and success. Choice also appeals to the brain's natural curiosity and increases intrinsic goal motivation (Cordova & Lepper, 1996).

As you gradually begin to offer choice, you'll find what boundaries and parameters your students need as individuals and as a class. Choice returns responsibility for learning to the students and builds their executive functions of judgment and decision making. Some students, especially Map Readers, may feel anxious about having too much freedom, fearing they won't do the right thing. By starting with small choices first, however, students will develop the skills of making and following through on appropriate and pleasurable choices.

Here are some additional motivating benefits of choice:

- Homework assignments or tests that begin with problems that the students select are reassuring—students feel that they know how to approach the problems; the confidence builds optimism, dopamine, focus, and perseverance; and the process creates a positive, confident beginning.
- Choice can allow students to approach an assignment through their learning strengths and most successful personal strategies.
- When choices include connections to the real, "here-me-now" world of the students, their development of intrinsic reward increases due to the satisfaction of doing something they value.
- As a teacher, you learn more about how to motivate individual students in the future by observing and noting their choices. When a unit is particularly tough for a student, your student profile card reminds you of his or her past choices and preferences, and you can include those in the day's opening. Similarly, observing past choices helps you guide advanced students to enrichment activities they will be motivated to do.

Here are some specific ways to provide motivating choices in math units:

- Encourage students to use sketches, sample problems, or various graphic organizers in their notes.
- Allow students to choose to complete the odd problems, even problems, or every third problem in their homework assignments.
- Have students choose from various presentation formats: PowerPoint, Web page, diagram, video, skit, chart, overhead projector, book (written for younger students, for example), graphs, or Excel spreadsheets.
- Allow students to choose work centers based on challenge level, interest, or readiness.
- Have students choose math-related games or activities they want to play in class.

Individualizing Long-Term Goal Setting

As you increase your knowledge of your students' achievable-challenge levels, learning strengths, and interests, you will be able to help them continue to grow as independent learners by extending the amount of delay their brains tolerate in terms of immediate gratification and the delayed intrinsic pleasure of more extended goal achievement. Young students don't have much gratification-delay wiring in the prefrontal cortex of their pleasure-seeking brain, so getting them to set longer-term goals requires much more convincing than short-term goal setting over the course of a class or a short unit.

Modeling is critical for your students to learn how to set and plan long-term goals. This is one of the reasons you show them your learning goals for a unit from the start and explain how steps along the way, such as homework, projects, and assessments, help you reach your outcome goal. Once they see how you start with a concrete outcome you expect to achieve, and how you plan to assess progress toward that outcome along the way, they have a sense of what goal planning looks like.

As you help students incorporate choice, personal interest, learning strengths, and executive function into selecting personal goals, they need background knowledge. They need to know *your* goals about what you expect *them* to learn and, for older students, how your lesson plans also incorporate the imposed goals set by the standards. This helps older students know that you may not have personally set (or like) every goal you must achieve. Sharing your opinions helps students realize that some goals are not ones they like, but ones they need to reach regardless. They recognize that you also face this problem and do so with a good attitude. Suddenly, they no longer think that the negative feelings are theirs alone, and they see that even if something is not pleasurable, they can get through these parts for the sake of a desirable end goal.

Without a personal investment, students can't control the RAS intake or the amygdala's conductor to admit and send information to their higher-thinking brains. Students need to develop goals they *want* to achieve based on the information you show and tell them about what the unit has to offer and what your goals for them include.

GRAY MATTER

Building Goal-directed Behavior

Much of what is considered goal-directed behavior, in terms of the qualities described in successful students, emphasizes the brain's prefrontal executive functions. When students are able to learn in low-stress environments with frequent and supportive feedback, appropriate challenge, and choice, they will be in the state in which the RAS and amygdala will be most likely to prime their brains to receive new information, connect it with existing stored memory, and form relational memory patterns that can then be used for the higher cognitive function of goal-directed behavior.

The behaviors (for students to practice and teachers to reinforce) to build these executive functions—such as focus, prioritization, organization, critical analysis, interpretation of emotions, and judgment—are those that build students' skills at self-monitoring and self-discipline. Strong intrinsic attraction to goals increases students' motivation to achieve those goals—all the more reason to incorporate choice and students' personally valued goals into the required academic goals of each unit.

✤ STRATEGY: Individualize Goals

The setup for a successful math unit and math year is working out individual plans for goal setting and achieving. As we have seen, individualized goal setting increases relevance and engagement for students. When you work with your students to create their learning goals, they are more likely to recognize and care about the correlation between their efforts and the results of those efforts. Students need guidance to find a personal interest goal that relates to the academic goal of the lesson. It is then a matter of helping them realize that the knowledge you have to offer is valuable to build and transfer to achieve their goals. These interventions remove the negativity regarding new learning that your students have built up over the previous years as a result of superficial levels of memorizing and using math facts and procedures just to answer test questions.

Once you have presented your global opening for your first long-term goal lesson, activate the dormant circuits of positive math feelings and curiosity your students once had. Ask them to describe a time when they were excited about and interested in a lesson or unit in any class. Let them know that this is what you want to help them feel about the current math unit.

Begin by filling out KWL charts, and then move on to a discussion of positive emotions students recall from previous learning experiences. Explain that you will help each student find ways to bring back those experiences of learning with pleasure. Be honest and clear that not everything will be fun; ask if there were perhaps some parts of previous learning experiences that were boring or frustrating but worth it in the end.

Bring up an example of a new puppy (or any pet). Did anyone ever get a new puppy? Was there anything they needed to prepare so the house was ready for the puppy? Were there things they needed to learn about caring for the puppy? Were there things they had to do for the puppy that were not fun at all, such as walking him early in the morning before school or cleaning up after him? Was it worth it? Relate these experiences to getting new math knowledge. Students will put in work to get the foundational knowledge they need to own the math concept, but just like caring for a puppy, the hard work in the beginning will provide this ownership for the rest of their lives. (My students have even plugged away through the challenges and tedium of drills by joking, "Oh well, it's just a little puppy poop.")

✤ STRATEGY: Infuse Goals with Optimism

Once you've opened with applications of the topic that have "here-me-now," real-world value to your students—so there is something they *want* to learn from the unit—have them discuss as a group (and, if old enough, write down) what their goals or dreams are, without limits based on what seems realistic now.

Discuss what they hope to learn in this unit to help them reach their goals (they have the KWL chart for cues). Write down their ideas. Next, have a discussion about what they might include in a plan to reach their goals and the unit goals. Share your optimism with validating comments such as "I see in you a student who will do [one of their goals or dreams] someday" or "I know you've worked hard on the [basketball court, school play, band, bake sale, etc.] to reach that goal. I know you have it in you to reach this goal too."

Have students write a few words or sketch something that represents their dreams. Put these up on a bulletin board under the title "Our Dreams, Our Motivators," and encourage students to look at those dreams when they need motivation to persevere over the long haul.

Optimism influences learning success, which in turn increases dopamine and encourages more learning. Using these visions of the future as personal connections to what your students will learn adds positive expectancy to the way they relate to the unit. This positive attitude changes their brain neurochemistry, and the dopamine release increases their responsiveness to and memory of the new material.

✤ STRATEGY: Apply Achievable Challenge to Goal Setting

When your students have established their goals and identified the steps required to achieve them, it is time to meet with each student to create an individual plan with achievable challenge. You can prepare for these meetings by planning potential alternative approaches for individual projects, inquiries, investigations, fundamental skills requirements, and homework assignments that you design to help students progress to the unit goals. When you meet, use students' own goals, strengths, interests, and existing foundational knowledge to guide them in planning their routes of achievable challenges. In other words, cocreate their plans for success. You can then extend your students' executive-function skills and help them commit to their plans by asking, "How are you going to know that you're progressing on track? How will you monitor and demonstrate your progress along the way?"

Because you are collaborating to reach connected goals, and the students have personally meaningful individual goals, the route of achievable challenge, along with a rubric, will guide the organization of their plans. Rubrics are frameworks that provide students with direction for successfully accomplishing their assignments and reaching their goals. Rubrics offer differentiated levels of mastery for the skills and concepts students need to master. By helping students select their appropriate-challenge level on the four, five, or six achievement measurements on the rubric, you are able to give them structure and choice in planning for success.

Rubric-based grading can be especially useful to keep the bar high and challenge level appropriate. Rubrics offer flexibility in that they include several categories that can be rated, such as quality of work, organization, ability to follow the assignment instructions, ability to meet deadlines, effort, creativity, prioritization, judgment, analysis, and proper use of resources. Using rubrics, students can see which areas of weakness need further practice and which rubric areas they can apply their strengths to in order to achieve the highest level of success. Rubrics provide direction throughout the unit as well as specific feedback about improvement, areas of specific strengths, and challenges that need further work.

For most students, the rubric will likely have at least one category in which they feel capable of achieving the highest level. More advanced math students can be encouraged to strive for an added level labeled "Advanced" or "Honors." Rubrics provide the same opportunities for all students while offering flexibility that accommodates individual achievable challenge in multiple components of mathematics. Because rubrics demonstrate the relationship between student work, attitude, effort, and measurement of their improvement and achievement, they are powerful tools that use the brain's dynamics of predictability and patterning to guide and assess effort with respect to the number of possible areas of achievement offered on the rubric.

Motivating for Goal-Directed Learning

The ability of children to delay gratification for the sake of later, more valued outcomes is related to success in mathematics and all subsequent scholastic performance (Mischel, Shoda, & Rodriguez, 1989). Your students' math negativity may have deprived them of experiencing the rewards of delayed gratification, especially regarding effort applied to mathematics. Collaborating with them on goal-motivated learning, with codeveloped desirable goals and graphs that link efforts and goals, gives your students the experience of connecting effort and progress. Your math class can be the place where students develop the goal-directed motivation, organizational skills, and perseverance that will serve them in situations beyond school and that will last for the rest of their lives.

GRAY MATTER

The Marshmallow Test

The Marshmallow Test was an experiment that measured a preschooler's ability to delay gratification in order to receive a greater reward. Four-year-old children were given a marshmallow and told they could have another if they resisted eating the first for 20 minutes. Those who could delay gratification and wait for the second marshmallow often developed into "more dependable" adolescents, and they generally scored higher on the SATs (Shoda, Mischel, & Peake, 1990). The children that did not eat the marshmallow and accepted the two later were named "resisters," and those that ate the single marshmallow were labeled "impulsives."

Impulsives were found to become adults who were more troubled, stubborn, indecisive, mistrustful, less self-confident, and still not able to put off gratification. During their later education years, they had trouble delaying immediate impulses to achieve long-range goals and were easily distracted by more pleasurable activities, even when they knew they needed to study for a test or write a report. As adults, they reported less successful marriages, lower job satisfaction and income, poorer health, and more frustration in their lives.

Resisters became successful students and eventually grew into fulfilled adults. In addition, the Marshmallow Test of delayed gratification was twice as accurate a predictor of later SAT scores than the subjects' IQ scores. Resisters scored an average of 210 more points (out of 1,600 total points) on SAT tests (Sethi, Mischel, Aber, Shoda, & Rodriguez, 2000).

Subsequent analysis revealed that, more than IQ tests, the capacity for sustained work, concentration, effort, steadiness of purpose, and persistence were the characteristics shared by exemplary students in science, math, sports, and music. This relationship between deliberate practice appears to be causal and not simply correlational (Ericsson, 1996).

Angela Duckworth carried out a similar analysis after leaving her job as an algebra teacher and becoming a psychologist. She had reached a point in which she concluded that trying to teach students without self-control was both frustrating and futile. In one research project, she found that the ability to delay gratification (8th graders were given a choice between a dollar right away or two dollars the following week) was a far better predictor of academic performance than IQ and concluded that intelligence is important, but it's not as important as self-control (Duckworth & Seligman, 2005).

♣ STRATEGY: Use Effort-Goal Graphs

Students taught about the relationship between effort and success become the highest achievers and are even more successful than students who are taught techniques for time management and comprehension of new material (Van Overwalle & De Metsenaere, 1990). Creating effort-goal graphs shows students a concrete way that their efforts will result in progress toward achieving their personal (and your academic) goals. Ideally, students make their own graphs, choosing styles and colors, but the graphs can be teacher-made and colored in by students as young as kindergartners. The purpose is for students to frequently see for themselves that time and practice result in progress toward and ultimate achievement of their goals.

Students (with help from a parent, if necessary) keep records and make bar graphs of the time spent on math or the amount of material reviewed each day, as well as weekly totals. Next to the weekly total, have students graph their grades that were based on the week's formal and informal assessments.

If a specific foundational fact set or procedure students lack is something they also practice regularly (perhaps because they are behind in that area), that fact or procedure has its own graph that records time or amount of material practiced and the number of correct answers on a specific test of that information. The visible recognition of success on their graph and the increased comfort that accompanies increased comprehension build gradually, especially if your students have low self-esteem in math. To sustain motivation until the correlation becomes ingrained, you can promote intrinsic motivation with additional feedback.

Before starting the graph, relate the concept of improvement with effort to your students' experiences outside of school, drawing on examples such as practicing basketball shots, a musical instrument, keyboarding, and video games. I've made recordings of students who start learning a musical instrument the year they are in my class. I record them playing three times during the year, and they estimate the amount of time they practiced. When I play these tapes to students in subsequent years, the effect is dramatic. I often use these recordings, without any explanation, as a novel way to open class early in the year. The students predict what they think they heard and are often surprised that the same individual performed the three segments.

We then discuss our own experiences with effort-goal success in examples such as drawing a recognizable picture, riding a bicycle, swimming, or using the computer. Because these are things that happen at approximately the same time for most children and are not considered unique skills, students usually do not register the process that links effort to success. In addition, the part of the brain that makes these correlations and predictions is the prefrontal cortex, the last part of the brain to mature, in a process that continues well into the 20s. What seems obvious to us as adults is not recognized as a pattern by children's young brains without explicit evidence.

At first, the goals need to be broken down into small measures of progress on the way to the main goal or students will not have the dopamine-reward feedback to persevere with the effort and the extra work of recording the data. Until they see results and hear about their classmates' experiences for several weeks, their brains will not develop new neural pathways to replace the automatic default pathways they've built up over years of negative experiences.

Once students have heard the "musician" in the music-practice example and acknowledged their own effort-success experiences, they are typically motivated to try the graphs. The data collection and time spent helping students create and understand their graphs is imposing at first, but it is certainly worth the investment. Encourage students to share the results of their graphs and their personal responses to what they discover.

What should be included on the graphs? For older students, additional data are useful once they see the most critical correlation between effort and progress. Depending on challenge areas and goals, students can have differentiated goals and can include comments about amount of effort and efficiency of study time, level of class comfort, and strategies used. (Later they can also record which strategies were most successful—what worked?—and what they are going to do to improve.) When they are drilling (using tools such as errorless math cards), the data should include speed and accuracy as well as quiz results.

Eventually, their effort-progress graphs will reveal patterns about their best strategies for specific types of math goals and the kinds of feedback most successful for them. This knowledge adds to successful planning of future goals and goal-achievement strategies. Additional positive results occur when students journal, write letters for portfolios, or write letters to parents about their observations and positive feelings. They can also write versions of these letters for students who will be in your class the following year (always a motivator for the recipient and a reinforcement of success for the writer).

The power of this visual model is that students can see that their level of success is under their control. Children who seek to master an academic topic with mastery-oriented goals show better long-term academic development in mathematics than do their peers whose main goals are to get good grades or outperform others (U.S. Dept. of Education, 2008).

Students can savor successes and be acknowledged without having to be embarrassed by low scores or feel boastful about high scores because the measurement is of progress toward a goal, not of specific numbers. Instead of the more typical competitive list of scores for all students (using numbers or letter grades), acknowledge students by percentage of achievement toward an individual goal. Two students who each selected a goal of mastering different segments of the multiplication tables (through the 5s and 9s, for example) can each get 100 percent *achievement,* even though they both mastered different material.

How can you support students' progress? Once students start on the effort-to-goal pathway, they still need your help to persevere. You can provide support with periodic meetings, feedback, acknowledgment of effort, reinforcement of self-appreciation, and lessons based on the Brain Owner's Manual (see Appendix B).

To help your students frame their math goals for the unit, and for remediation of background knowledge that is missing, you can provide formal and informal formative assessment during individual meetings. When you frequently evaluate their learning and offer corrective feedback while they are still involved in charting their progress, they can, with your encouragement, make adjustments along the route to their final goals—before units or projects are completed or tests are taken.

When you meet with students, first ask them to reflect on their progress. What changes have they noticed? What is now easy that once was hard? What have they discovered about how they learn and study for the best results? After they respond, supply feedback based on your observations of their work and knowledge of their strengths. Make suggestions and remind them of the tools that will move them toward their goals in the most efficient manner.

The way you acknowledge students' effort influences their expectations of success. Praising students for the effort reflected in movement toward their goals keeps them engaged. When you acknowledge their effort along the way using "minigoals" (short-term goals that are made evident to students as steps toward the long-term goal), they recognize early on that their progress is related to their perseverance. These meetings motivate students to continue to use effort to persevere through challenge and to apply what they learn to new problems. They gradually build resilience and even enjoyment of challenge.

Specific, sincere, supportive interest in and response to students' progress, not just attainment of their final goals, is a major component of these meetings. Be sure to end by drawing attention to the parts of their graphs that show evidence of their progress, and comment on that evidence. For example, say, "That's great. You earned it. I'm so proud of you!"

What will you notice? The effort-progress graphs are the first step for student development of delayed gratification. The ability to relate effort to success gives your students a way to predict and therefore take control of their math future. They see, perhaps for the first time, the positive connection between their actions and resulting consequences. They understand that effort over time pays off, which motivates them *now* and increases their tolerance of frustration that is related to occasional setbacks and to the "fast and heavy" curriculum demands that require continual memorization of facts.

It will take time and patience to develop students' neural circuits that connect long-term goals to required intermediate steps, new-skill acquisition, and practice. When students have a cycle of failure, the network of negativity is strong and becomes a powerful self-fulfilling prophecy with each additional failure. Strengthened through repeated stimulation and neuroplasticity, the new, positive networks will become students' default and will give them the ability to show resilience. When setbacks take place, going back to their effort-progress graphs will put the setback in perspective.

You may find your students are ready to extend their PFC executive functions and develop more personal responsibility, control of emotional responses, planning skills, problem-solving skills, and self-motivation. You can take their newfound discovery of the connection between effort and progress and help them continue to learn to regulate the functions of numbers and of their own behavior by looking for patterns and connections to prior knowledge and experience, anticipating the consequences of their actions, planning or predicting into the future, using organizational skills, and applying effort to achieve goals.

Consider reading the preceding paragraph again. If you read it with student self-directed control in mind, now read it in relation to solving math problems, or vice versa. It fascinates me that the concepts that drive success in mathematics and the way that the brain is programmed to process big mathematical ideas and patterns are essentially the same as the development of executive function and personal responsibility in humans. It can all come together in your classroom!

—————————————————

You know why *you* believe math is important, but what is obvious to you is not necessarily evident to your students. They may know the isolated facts but haven't made the connections to link isolated facts into memory patterns that have the predictive power to inform their insight and decisions. Remember that an immature prefrontal cortex and gaps in students' concept development prevent the hippocampus from linking appropriate prior knowledge with new information.

You may be the only person your students spend time with who has a positive attitude about math. When they respect you, they want to be like you. Demonstrate through your words, actions, and emotions that you value mathematical thinking and why you love math and want to share your knowledge with them.

Conclusion

By now, you have learned that the knowledge gained from brain research, when applied to learning, can help you energize and enliven your students' minds. As their teacher, you can help them build life skills such as improved memory, focus, organization, and goal setting. Using the brain-friendly strategies best suited for your students' learning strengths, they will build aptitude and confidence in math (and all school subjects) and become lifelong learners who can transfer and apply what they learn to real-world situations.

Before children can love math, they have to be comfortable with it. If it is perceived as threatening, they will resist. When you help students feel confident that you will work with them so they can use their learning strengths, they will persevere with effort to achieve meaningful goals, feel safe taking risks in a supportive class community, and learn from their mistakes.

When the learning environment in your math classroom provides stability and familiarity, with comfortable class routines and respectful classroom behaviors (all good for the amygdala), as well as novel and pleasurable activities (good for the reticular activating system and the release of dopamine), your students will build comfort with and an interest in math. With lessons that are engaging, personally meaningful, and suitably differentiated to offer achievable challenge, your students' math anxieties and phobias will be replaced by confidence, and their success in mathematics will rise to meet your expectations.

When children passively take in information to regurgitate on standardized tests, they are experiencing little actual learning. For their brains to process information so that it can be stored in their long-term memory banks, they must actively manipulate it. In mathematics, you help your students do this by having them use the information to investigate, classify, categorize, compare, contrast, or solve challenging problems using their higher-level thinking skills. Information you present through multisensory experiences, personalization, and achievable-challenge progression connects your students with mathematics in a positive way that will influence their future learning.

Individualized goal setting increases relevance and engagement for your students. When you allow students to join you in creating learning goals, they are more likely to recognize and care about the correlation between their efforts and the goal-achieving results of those efforts, especially when you guide your students to find their own interest-related goals to relate to the academic goal of the lesson. Your students will develop conceptual understanding that they can apply and transfer to new situations beyond the superficial level of memorizing and using facts and procedures to answer test questions.

My final bit of advice is directed to you, the teacher. The message is simple: Revel in your successes and not your less-successful ventures. Know that when you help your students develop skills, strategies, and attainment of higher levels of thinking, they become increasingly engaged in learning in and out of school. Their self-confidence increases, and they are now more resilient when they encounter obstacles and frustrations. They know they can accomplish anything they set their minds to because they have done just that in your class. You have dedicated yourself to making a difference in the lives of your students, and because of that, you have changed the future.

Appendix A: Internet Resources

The following resources were accurate at the time of publication. Keep in mind, however, that many online resources change or are discontinued, so they need to be checked before recommending them to students, parents, or colleagues.

✤ Activities, Projects, and Worksheets for Teachers

A to Z Teacher Stuff®
http://atozteacherstuff.com

CSI: Mathematics, Curriculum Support Information
www.ceismc.gatech.edu/CSI

Education Planet®
www.educationplanet.com

Education World®
www.educationworld.com

The Educator's Reference Desk[sm]: Lesson Plans
http://askeric.org/Virtual/Lessons

Learner.org
www.learner.org

LessonPlanz.com™
www.lessonplanz.com

Math Worksheet Generator
www.mccollam.com/math

National Council of Teachers of Mathematics: Illuminations
http://illuminations.nctm.org

RubiStar (*printable rubric templates*)
http://rubistar.4teachers.org

Teacher Planet®: Lesson Plans for Teachers
www.lessonplans4teachers.com

♣ *Games / Fact Practice*

A to Z Investments: History of Wall Street and the Stock Markets
www.atozinvestments.com/more-wall-street-history.html

AAA Math (*K–8 interactive arithmetic lessons*)
www.aaamath.com

Aplus Math (*K–8 interactive arithmetic games and worksheets*)
http://aplusmath.com/Games/index.html

British Nutrition Foundation (*conversion tables and recipes*)
www.foodafactoflife.org.uk/Sheet.aspx?siteId=12&sectionId=49&content
Id=131

Cool Math® (*K–8 interactive arithmetic games*)
www.coolmath.com

Cool Math 4 Kids® (*8–12 interactive arithmetic games*)
www.coolmath4kids.com

DimensionM (*online multiplayer video games where K–12 students compete and collaborate with other players*)
www.dimensionu.com/math

Discovery Education®: Brain Boosters
http://school.discoveryeducation.com/brainboosters/#number

Explore Learning: Gizmos™ (*interactive online simulations for grades 3–12*)
www.explorelearning.com

Inter*activate*: Activities (*K–8 interactive arithmetic games and worksheets*)
www.shodor.org/interactivate/activities

Inter*activate*: Area Explorer (*interactive activities about area calculation*)
www.shodor.org/interactivate/activities/AreaExplorer

Kinderweb Educational Children's Games
(*PreK–6 interactive arithmetic games*)
http://kinderwebgames.com

Knowledge Matters: Virtual Business Challenge (*business and financial literacy simulations*)
http://vbc.knowledgematters.com/vbc/sports/about

Learner.org: Cooking by Numbers (*metric recipes*)
www.learner.org/interactives/dailymath/meters_liters.html

The MAA Mathematical Sciences Digital Library (*links to math news, events, and free game sites*)
http://mathdl.maa.org

Math Cats: Tessellation Town (*tessellation activities*)
www.mathcats.com/explore/tessellationtown.html

Math Fact Cafe™: The Fact Sheet Factory (*K–8 math games, flash cards, and worksheets*)
www.mathfactcafe.com

The Math Forum @ Drexel (*sports-themed activities*)
http://mathforum.org/library/topics/sports

Math Jokes
www.sonoma.edu/Math/faculty/falbo/jokes.html

Mathletics! (*sports-related math games*)
http://chalk.richmond.edu/education/projects/webunits/math/sport.html

Natural Math (*math and nature activities*)
www.naturalmath.com

NCTM Illuminations (*math games for grades 6–8*)
http://illuminations.nctm.org/Activities.aspx?grade=3

PBS Kids Lesson Plan: Play the Market (*stock market math game*)
http://pbskids.org/bigapplehistory/parentsteachers/business_lesson7.html

Puzzle Pixies (*K–8 interactive games*)
www.puzzlepixies.com/medium/medium/sherlocks-secret-code.html

SuperKids® Math Worksheet Creator (*math worksheets, games, quotes, and vocabulary*)
www.superkids.com/aweb/tools/math

Tessellation World of Makoto Nakamura
http://makoto-nakamura.sakura.ne.jp/home.index.html

Tessellations.org
www.tessellations.org

Texas Instruments: Classroom Activities (*math activities for children in grades K–12; calculator activities for all ages*)
http://education.ti.com/educationportal/sites/US/sectionHome/classroomactivities.html

U.S. Department of Education: Helping Your Child Learn Mathematics (*activities that parents can use with children from preschool through grade 5 to strengthen math skills and build strong positive attitudes*)
www.ed.gov/parents/academic/help/math/index.html

Universal Currency Converter
www.xe.com/ucc

Wolfram MathWorld™ (*links to math games, terms, lessons for grades 8–12*)
http://mathworld.wolfram.com/about

✤ Graphic Organizers

edHelper Graphic Organizers (*printable graphic organizers*)
www.edhelper.com/teachers/graphic_organizers.htm

Education Place Graphic Organizers (Houghton Mifflin Harcourt) (*printable graphic organizers*)
www.eduplace.com/graphicorganizer

Freeology.com (*printable graphic organizers*)
http://freeology.com/graphicorgs

Graphic.org Graphic Organizers (*printable graphic organizers*)
www.graphic.org/goindex.html

Kidspiration®: Grades K–5 (*visual learning to build conceptual understanding in math*)
www.inspiration.com/kidspiration

National Library of Virtual Manipulatives (*visual learning opportunities for math*)
http://nlvm.usu.edu/en/nav/topic_t_5.html

NCES Kids' Zone: Create a Graph (*elementary school graphing activities*)
http://nces.ed.gov/nceskids/createagraph/default.aspx

TeacherVision®: Lesson Plans, Printables, and More (*printable graphic organizers and lesson plans*)
www.teachervision.fen.com/graphic-organizers/printable/6293.html

✤ Instruction and Assessment

ALEKS® (*system for math practice and corrective feedback*)
www.aleks.com

CTB/McGraw-Hill: Acuity™ (*formative assessment tool*)
www.acuityforschool.com

✤ Videos and Activities

The Futures Channel® (*videos and lessons for real-world math and science applications*)
www.thefutureschannel.com/hands-on_math.php

Appendix B: Brain Owner's Manual

During the first four weeks of school, I present three 15-minute sessions focused on this material. I explain a section of the material in my own words and demonstrate with models, sketches, or actual images of brain structures. Students' questions usually prompt discussion that deepens their understanding of the brain's functions. I also ask questions that increase their curiosity. For example, I might ask, "Why don't neurons (nerve cells in the brain) replace themselves like skin and blood cells do?" Students are typically puzzled and curious by this. Eventually, they recognize that learning and practice are needed for information to become memories stored in neurons; if brains continually replaced neurons, learned information would be lost.

As we learn about brain function, students draw sketches or make clay models that represent their growing dendrites. I encourage all students to discuss and/or write about how this new information influences their attitudes toward school, their study habits, and their ability to change their own intelligence.

Throughout the year, I incorporate reminders about brain function into my instructional strategies. For example, when I introduce the summarizing benefits of dend-*writes,* I promote discussion about the growth of more dendrites in neural networks when new information that we learn, practice, and use is solidified into memory. When students complain about homework, I ask volunteers to read their notes or show their diagrams and explain how homework is an opportunity for their brains to rehearse newly learned information and stimulate dendrite growth.

Explaining to students how the brain functions—in terms of our ability to learn—can provide many benefits, including an increase in motivation, interest, and student understanding of the value of various learning strategies available to them (and why those strategies work). The following is an example of how you might present relevant information about the brain to students at the upper-elementary or middle school levels.

Learning takes place through a series of electrical and chemical events. Everything you learn comes to the brain through your senses. The brain itself doesn't have sensory nerves that feel pain (which is why some brain surgery can be done painlessly while the patient is awake and talking in order for the doctor to know which damaged parts of the brain can be safely removed). The sensory nerves in your skin, muscles, stomach, eyes, ears, nose, and taste buds all send information to the brain. This is how you "know" what you are seeing, hearing, feeling, smelling, or tasting.

The brain has obstacles to information getting in. These obstacles are filters that protect the brain from overload. The brain is an amazing organ, but it is not equipped to process the billions of bits of sensory information that bombard it every second! When your brain is calm and not stressed by emotions such as fear, anger, frustration, or sadness, you have more control and choice about which information from your environment gets into your brain and then travels into your conscious *reflective* brain. You can calm and focus your brain's intake center—the *reticular activating system* (RAS)—to control how your brain selects which sensory data to let in through the RAS filter. From those billions of bits of sensory information available, only about 2,000 bits can pass this RAS filter per second, and you can influence which information gets your attention and gets admitted to the higher brain. How well you *store* the sensory input that makes it through your brain filters is also influenced by your emotional state at the time you hear, see, and experience the sensory information and the way you prepare your brain to receive new information by activating memories about things you already know.

When your brain filters work optimally—because your stress levels are down and your interest is high—the most valuable information can pass into your memory and your thinking brain. When you are anxious, worried, sad, frustrated, confused, or bored, your brain filters often conduct sensory information from the world around you into the automatic systems of your brain. These *reactive,* automatic brain systems can select three things to do with the information—send signals that cause you to act out (*fight* against the negative experience), daydream or doodle (take *flight* away from the unpleasant experience), or ignore it (*freeze* it out). This is your reactive brain in a fight/flight/freeze mode.

Developing awareness of your own emotions and personal strengths empowers you to respond to the most important sensory input (information) from your environment. Practicing, reviewing, and doing something with what you learn (mental manipulation) makes the memory circuits in your brain stronger so you can keep what you learn in your long-term memory and use the knowledge to solve problems and be creative.

Your Brain Is RAD

Three main brain components are the keys to control over the information that your brain takes in and processes. They operate through your highest thinking and reasoning abilities, which are based in your prefrontal cortex (PFC), a thin layer of neurons in the front of your brain and behind your eyes. The three components are what I refer to as RAD, which is short for

Reticular Activating System (RAS)
Amygdala
Dopamine

♣ Reticular Activating System (RAS)

Information enters the brain as sensory data (from what you hear, see, smell, touch, or taste). To enter your brain, this sensory information must first pass through the reticular activating system and later through the limbic system (especially the *amygdala* and the *hippocampus*) to be acknowledged, recognized, coded into patterns, and ultimately stored in long-term memory.

The RAS is an attention-switching system located at the lower back of your brain (*brainstem*). The RAS receives input from the body's sensory nerves that converge into the spinal cord from sensory-response nerve endings in the eyes, ears, mouth, other parts of the face, skin, muscles, and internal organs. These sensory messages must first pass through the RAS filter to either (1) gain entry to the higher, thinking, *reflective* prefrontal cortex brain or (2) be sent directly to the automatic, reflexive, *reactive* response centers.

The goal for successful learning and emotional control is to keep the RAS filter open to the flow of information that you want to enter your PFC. The more stress you feel, the harder it is for you to focus attention, create memories in your reflective brain, and use what you learn to do well on tests and be a creative problem solver. If you are overwhelmed and feel out of control, your automatic brain takes over and what you experience, focus on, and remember is not in your control. If you build your power to focus your attention on the sensory input that is most valuable and important to attend to at the moment, *you* are in control. The difference between the two states is the difference between *reflecting* and *reacting* to your world—in other words, being in control of rather than controlled by outside influences.

You can strengthen your ability to choose the way your brain senses things around you by focusing, practicing self-observation, and recognizing how your effort influences your ability to reach your goals. If you make the decision to review and practice what you learn, you grow the parts of your brain that make your memories permanent.

♣ Your Amygdala—Where Your Heart Meets Your Mind

The brain is divided into lobes, each with specialized functions and connections to other lobes. These connections create networks of cell-to-cell communication for your more complex brain activities. If the sensory information you see, hear, feel, smell, or touch gets through the RAS, it travels to sensory intake centers of your brain. The areas most active when new information first comes into the brain are the *sensory cortex areas* in each specialized lobe of your brain. Each lobe is specialized to analyze data from one sense.

This new sensory input is then identified and classified as your brain matches it with neuron networks you already have constructed with memories that relate to the new information. For example, the sight of a lemon connects with patterns stored in the visual cortex in your *occipital* lobes.

The sensory recognition networks in your *parietal* lobes recognize the feel of the lemon.

To reach your PFC, the sensory data that passed through your RAS must now pass through your brain's emotional core (the *limbic system*), especially your amygdala and hippocampus, where emotional meaning is linked to information. For example, the sour taste of lemons is delicious in lemon sherbet but unpleasant in unsweetened lemon juice. Once the sensory data are received, these emotional filters evaluate their survival value and pleasure value.

Helping Information Flow Through Your Amygdala. Try to recall "one of those days" when the morning got off to a bad start. You overslept and had no time for breakfast, and you had many things to do before school. You got to school but worried if your friends would be with you at lunch or if another student in your class would say hurtful things. What you might not realize is that if you didn't get enough sleep or have a nutritious breakfast, it is not only your body that suffers. Your brain is also stressed and less attentive, so you do not get the most out of your day at school. This happens because stress closes off the pathways through the RAS and amygdala that direct information into reflective thinking and memory in your PFC.

For example, when you are bored by a lesson (because you already know how to do long division, for example) or frustrated (because you are confused by the difficult vocabulary words in the story the class is reading), your amygdala's filter responds to the stress by taking up excessive amounts of your brain's available nutrients and oxygen. Your brain is now in "survival mode." This high activity in your amygdala blocks entry of information to your thinking brain, so the knowledge being presented will never make it to your PFC.

The amygdala filter is like a switching mechanism on train tracks. If you are stressed or very confused and frustrated, your brain will be in survival mode and the amygdala will send the information into the automatic, reactive brain. If you are calm, alert, and focused, your amygdala filters will make the "decision" to send the information to your thinking brain in the PFC.

In addition, if the learning situation is one that is enjoyable and you feel good during the lesson, the amygdala will add a neurochemical enhancement, like a memory chip, to strengthen the information's staying power when it is later stored in memory. In a positive emotional state, you will learn and remember more of what you hear and read and be able to have more control of your emotions, reasoning, and creativity.

Making Memories That Last. Next to the amygdala in the limbic system is the hippocampus. It is in this coding center that new sensory input is linked to memories of your past experiences and things you already know that are pulled in from your memory storage. The newly coded relational memories, made of the new information linked to your existing memories, are now ready for processing in the prefrontal cortex.

There are highly developed nerve communication networks in your prefrontal cortex where creative, reflective, smarter thinking takes place. When the filters do not block the sensory information from what you hear, see, feel, and otherwise sense, the information can reach your higher-brain-function PFC regions. These higher-thinking reflective networks process the new information through what are called *executive functions* including judgment, analysis, organization, problem solving, planning, and creativity.

It is also in the executive function networks of your prefrontal cortex that short-term, coded relational memories of new information can become long-term memories. When you can focus your alertness and use self-monitoring to evaluate and control your emotional state, your PFC can actively process new information and your executive functions are most successful at organizing new information into long-term knowledge.

Practice Makes Permanent. Each time you review, remember, and practice something you learned, the mental manipulation increases the activity along the connections between nerve cells in the network that holds that memory. The repeated stimulation makes the network stronger—practice makes permanent—just like your muscles become stronger when you exercise them. In your brain, new sprouts called *dendrites* actually grow as branches from one nerve cell to the next when you practice a memory. The more connections that form and the more frequently they are stimulated, the stronger the memory becomes, the longer it will stay in your brain, and the easier it will be to remember when you need it.

With enough practice, other branches in the memory network actually bulk up. Branches called *axons,* which carry information away from the neuron, get a thicker coating called *myelin.* Myelin is like insulation in a wire that conducts electricity better than a wire without insulation. When there are lots of dendrites—and the axons have nice, thick myelin—the memory becomes more permanent because this neural circuit is stronger. Imagine how great it will be when your memory of the multiplication tables is as permanent and automatic as your memory of how to ride a bike!

When you review new learning in active ways, using the knowledge or procedure to do or create something, solve problems, or apply it to another subject, this mental manipulation strengthens the neural pathways and your brain becomes more efficiently wired. This process, called *neuroplasticity*, means that the practice that stimulates the useful brain networks actually makes them stronger and more efficient.

Your own mental efforts in all types of executive functions (higher thinking), such as delaying immediate gratification, working to achieve goals, and evaluating the strategies you used when you were most successful, actually build your brain into a more efficient and successful tool that you control. You become the sculptor of your brain's PFC nerve circuits that focus your attention, retain information in long-term memory, and retrieve the stored knowledge you need to solve new problems in your academic and emotional life. There is strong overlap in the PFC networks of emotional control and intelligent thinking. As you exercise (stimulate) these networks, you'll find that when you stop to evaluate your emotional feelings the way you analyze problems in math or skills in soccer, your stronger PFC nerve circuits will better enable you to manage frustration, confusion, or boredom instead of letting these feelings control you.

♣ Dopamine and Pleasure

Dopamine is one of the brain's most important *neurotransmitters*. Some of the other neurotransmitters in the brain include serotonin, tryptophan, acetylcholine, and norepinephrine. Remember that your brain holds tiny bits of information in neurons in the cerebral cortex. These nerve cells communicate with other neurons to send messages by branches (axons and dendrites) that almost touch the branches of the next neuron. Axons carry the information away from a neuron, and dendrites bring the message to the next neuron. It takes lots of connections to relate each neuron's tiny bit of information to other neurons so all the bits can add up to a complete memory.

There are gaps between axons and dendrites called *synapses.* Brain messages from neuron to neuron travel as tiny electric currents. Like electricity, these messages need wiring to carry them. There is no wiring at the synaptic gap, so the electrical messages are carried on chemical neurotransmitters (such as dopamine, serotonin, and acetylcholine). These neurotransmitters are brain proteins that carry information across the synapses.

When extra dopamine is released and travels to more parts of your brain, additional neurons are activated, expanding the good feelings. If you are unfocused, angry, or stressed, different neurotransmitters and chemicals, such as cortisol, spread through your brain, and negative feelings take control.

There are activities you can do to increase dopamine levels in your brain. Physical activity that you enjoy, interacting with friends, laughing, feeling an inner sense of reward for doing something well, achieving a personal goal, listening to someone read to you, and acting kindly have all been correlated with boosts in dopamine and pleasure.

Your brain even has a reward network, the nucleus accumbens, deep inside each side of your brain, which releases dopamine primarily into the PFC. Higher dopamine levels in the PFC correspond with increased feelings of satisfaction or pleasure. When this happens after your brain finds out it made a correct prediction, your personal strengths, talents, creativity, and motivation to persevere increase, even though you might make errors or have trouble finding the answer.

The boost in dopamine that comes from this reward network not only increases your own sense of pleasure, but it also increases other neurotransmitters, such as acetylcholine, that increase your alertness, focus, memory, and prefrontal cortex executive functions. You can then use your judgment and decision-making brainpower because *you* are in charge instead of the nonthinking, automatic, fight/flight/freeze parts of your brain.

Now you know that when dopamine is released during enjoyable learning activities, it actually increases your power to control attention and turn the learning into long-term memories. What will you do to have your brain release more dopamine to increase that sense of rewarding pleasure? What will you do to increase your ability to pay attention and remember things you want to remember?

Consider which experiences or activities give you that sense of accomplishment and pleasure associated with dopamine release. Think about your personal strengths, such as artistic ability, leadership, athletic skill, musical abilities, appreciation of nature, optimism, kindness, endurance, creativity, problem solving, or the ability to see the "big picture," notice details, and help friends or classmates resolve conflicts. Use these strengths to do things you want to do well. Put in effort and take time to acknowledge your progress in school or whatever you put your mind to, such as sports, art, music, or academics. The dopamine released during these activities and reflections is then available to further increase your attention, focus, creativity, and problem solving. It is a win-win situation: feel good and be smarter!

Take time to recognize how it feels when you experience the pleasure of self-satisfaction that occurs when your brain releases dopamine and acetylcholine. At those moments, these neurotransmitters are working together in your hippocampus, the memory-coding center next to your amygdala, to start the process of turning new information into coded messages that can travel to your PFC and be built into long-term memories. You can put this process into effect for learning. For example, if your vocabulary word practice includes enjoyable physical activity, such as acting out or drawing pictures of the meaning of the words, your brain will learn to associate vocabulary practice with pleasure. Studying becomes more efficient, easier, and faster, and the memories you make are more permanent.

Conclusion

By making the effort to achieve personally important goals using your strengths and the strategies and tools that work best for you, you can become the architect of your more intelligent, creative, and powerful brain. Add to this your emotional awareness—reflecting on your own feelings and those of others around you—and you will power the important learning information through your RAD system. Then the information can reach your PFC, and you can use your highest thinking skills (your reflective brain) to build long-term memories that you can call on when you need the information for a test or for anything you do.

Now you know that you hold the key that enables you to influence what information gets through your brain filters and how to mentally manipulate new learning to make memories permanent. If you think before you act, practice strategies you find valuable, and exercise your PFC executive functions and emotional control pathways, you can change your brain to be more successful at doing what you want to do and experience more pleasure in your academic and social pursuits.

You can *reflect* instead of *react* when you take a challenging test at school or when you face social conflicts with friends. The more you practice, the more your brain becomes a powerful tool that you control to reach your greatest learning and creative potential. You can reach your dreams and take the information you learn from teachers, parents, friends, books, and the world around you to become the wise and caring person you want to be and help create the world that will be best for all humanity.

Glossary

....

acetylcholine: A neurotransmitter that stimulates multiple brain centers, including the hippocampus, brainstem, and forebrain (where new learning takes place).

affective filter: A term referring to an emotional state of stress in students during which they are not responsive to processing, learning, and storing new information. This affective filter is represented by objective physical evidence on neuroimaging of the amygdala, which becomes metabolically hyperactive during periods of high stress. In this hyperstimulated state, new information does not pass through the amygdala to reach the prefrontal cortex information processing centers of the brain.

amygdala: Part of the limbic system in the brain's temporal lobe. It was first believed to function as a brain center for responding only to anxiety and fear. When the amygdala senses threat or high stress, it becomes overactivated; PET and fMRI scans show high metabolic activity represented by greatly increased radioactive glucose and oxygen use in the amygdala region. In students, these neuroimaging findings are seen when they feel helpless, stressed by boredom, and anxious. When the amygdala is in this state of stress, fear, anxiety-induced overactivation, or frustration from not understanding the lesson or reading, information coming through the sensory intake areas of the brain has limited access to be directed through the amygdala to the prefrontal cortex. Instead, input is directed to the lower, reactive brain, with behavior results such as fight/flight/freeze.

axon: The tiny fibrous extension of the neuron that conducts impulses away from the cell body to other target cells (e.g., neurons, muscles, glands).

brain mapping: A neuroscience technique of measuring electrical activity representing brain activation along neural pathways using electroencephalographic (EEG) response over time. This technique allows scientists to track which parts of the brain are active when a person is processing information at various stages of information intake, patterning, storing, and retrieval. The levels of activation in particular brain regions are associated with the intensity of information processing.

central nervous system: The portion of the nervous system consisting of the spinal cord and the brain.

cerebellum: A large structure located on top of the brainstem, resembling a cauliflower. This structure is very important for coordination, and it has the most links to the frontal lobe (compared to the other lobes).

cerebral cortex: The outermost layer of the cerebrum. The cortex has the highest proportion of neurons, which are darker in color than nerve fiber connections, such that this layer is also called "gray matter." The prefrontal cerebral cortex is a major component in executive functioning such as planning, problem solving, prioritizing, judgment, risk analysis, and conceptual and abstract thinking.

chunking: A learning strategy that enables students to remember more content more successfully. Because the working memory's capacity for immediate recall is believed to be limited to five to nine unrelated items, categorizing and sorting information into that number of chunks—rather than trying to memorize many discrete pieces of information—helps students internalize the material more effectively.

cognition: The mental process by which we become aware of our surroundings and use that information to solve problems and make sense out of the world.

computerized tomography (CT scan, CAT scan): A neuroimaging scan that uses a narrow beam of X-rays to create brain images displayed as a series of brain slices. To produce the image, a computer program estimates how much of the beam is absorbed in small areas within cross sections of the brain.

decoding sensory input: How the brain receives and makes sense of incoming information. Any new information or learning must enter the brain through one or more of the senses (hearing, seeing/visualizing, touching, tasting, smelling, and emotionally feeling). First, the information is received by the sense's specific sensory receptors. From there, the information travels to the reticular activating system just above the spinal cord, where it will either be admitted or edited out and essentially ignored.

dendrites: Branched protoplasmic extensions that carry information as electric signals to the axons or neuron cell body. A single neuron may possess thousands of dendrites. Dendrites increase in size and number in response to experience, information storage, and practiced, learned skills. Proteins called neurotrophins stimulate dendrite growth.

"dend-*write*": A nickname for an activity in which students summarize and record new information in their own words. This phrase refers to the fact that new learning—when physically established in the brain—is accompanied by the growth of more connections between nerve cells, called dendrites.

dopamine: A neurotransmitter most associated with satisfaction, pleasure, and intrinsic reward–stimulated learning. Neuroimaging has found that dopamine release increases in response to humor, movement, choice, positive interaction, music, and listening to stories read aloud.

EEG (electroencephalography): The neurophysiologic measurement of the electrical activity occurring from transmissions between neurons.

executive function: Cognitive processing of information that has significant direction from the prefrontal cortex. These executive functions—among the last brain processes to mature—include organizing, analyzing, sorting, connecting, planning, prioritizing, sequencing, self-monitoring, self-correcting, abstracting, problem solving, attention focusing, and linking information to appropriate actions.

functional brain imaging (neuroimaging): The use of techniques to directly or indirectly demonstrate the structure, function, or metabolic status of the brain. Whereas *structural* imaging reveals the overall structure of the brain, *functional* neuroimaging provides a visualization of the processing of information coming into the brain. This processing is visualized directly as areas of the brain "light up" through increased metabolism, blood flow, oxygen use, or glucose uptake.

functional magnetic resonance imaging (fMRI): A type of functional brain imaging that uses the paramagnetic properties of oxygen-carrying hemoglobin in the blood to demonstrate which brain structures are activated—and to what degree—during various performance and cognitive activities. Most fMRI research has subjects scanned while they are exposed to visual, auditory, tactile, or emotional stimuli and actively or passively respond to the input.

glia: Specialized cells that nourish, support, and complement the activity of neurons in the brain. Actrocytes are the most common and appear to play a key role in regulating the amount of neurotransmitters in the synapse by taking up excess neurotransmitters. Oligodendrocytes are glia that specialize to form the myelin sheath around many axonal projections.

gray matter: A term referring to the brownish-gray color of the parts of the brain and spinal cord with a high percentage of neurons (nerve cell bodies), in contrast to white matter, which is primarily composed of supportive tissue and connections between neurons.

hippocampus: A ridge in the floor of each lateral ventricle of the brain that consists mainly of gray matter and that has a major role in learning, memory, and emotional regulation. The hippocampus takes sensory inputs and integrates them with relational or associational patterns, thereby binding the separate aspects of the experience into storable patterns of relational memories.

hypothalamus: The part of the brain that lies below the thalamus and regulates body temperature, certain metabolic processes, and other autonomic activities that maintain the body at homeostasis (steady physiological state). The hypothalamus consists of a group of important nuclei that mediate many important functions. The hypothalamic nuclei are involved in regulating many of the body's internal organs via hormonal communication. The hypothalamus is a key part of the hypothalamic-pituitary-adrenal (HPA) axis that is so important in the stress response.

limbic system: A group of interconnected deep-brain structures involved in olfaction (smell), emotion, motivation, behavior, and various autonomic functions. Included in the limbic system are the thalamus, the amygdala, the hippocampus, and portions of the frontal and temporal lobes.

medial temporal lobe (MTL): The region on the inner side of each temporal lobe that connects with the prefrontal cortex in a circuit. The MTL, among other functions, is active in binding the separate elements of an experience into an integrated memory. This area of the brain includes several areas that are crucial for new memory formation, including the hippocampus.

metabolic hyperstimulation: The increased metabolism (biologic use) of oxygen or glucose to fuel nerve cells. When the limbic system, particularly the amygdala, is hyperstimulated by high stress, it becomes flooded by so much neural metabolic activity that new information cannot pass through it to the higher reasoning parts of the brain (such as the prefrontal cortex).

metacognition: Knowledge about one's own information processing and strategies that influence one's learning. After a lesson or an assessment, prompting students to reflect on the successful learning strategies that they used can help reinforce effective strategies and optimize future learning.

myelin: Fat-protein layers of insulation that surround the axons of many neurons. Myelin increases the speed of connections between brain regions, resulting in more efficient information access and retrieval.

neuronal circuits: Electrochemical connections through which neurons send coded communications to one another. When specific patterns of stimulation within the same group of neurons are stimulated repeatedly, their connecting circuit becomes more developed and more accessible to efficient stimulation and response. This is where practice (repeated stimulation of grouped neuronal connections in neuronal circuits) results in more successful memory storage and recall.

neurons: Specialized cells in the brain and throughout the nervous system that store tiny parts of a memory individually. When connected together by axon and dendrite links, they communicate and retain memory.

neurotransmitters: Brain proteins that transport information across synapses and also circulate throughout the brains. Neurotransmitters involved in synaptic transmissions are released by the electrical impulses on one side of the synapse and then float across the synaptic gap, carrying the information with them to stimulate the next nerve ending in the pathway. Once the neurotransmitter is taken up by the next nerve ending, the electric impulse is reactivated to travel along to the next nerve. Neurotransmitters in the brain include serotonin, acetylcholine, dopamine, and others. When neurotransmitters are depleted by too much information traveling through a nerve circuit without a break, the speed of transmission along the nerve slows down to a less efficient level.

neurotrophins (nerve growth factor): Proteins that stimulate growth of nerve cells. During sleep, neurotrophins are released in greater amounts, and there is an associated increase in the formation of new dendrites branching between neurons.

nucleus accumbens: A brain region above the brainstem involved in functions relating to motivation and intrinsic reward, especially by the release of dopamine into the prefrontal cortex when the person becomes aware of a correct prediction or decision.

occipital lobes (visual memory areas): Posterior lobes of the brain that process optical input, among other functions.

parietal lobes: Lobes on each side of the brain that process sensory data, locations, reading activities, and other functions.

patterning: The process whereby the brain perceives sensory data and generates patterns by relating new information with previously learned material, or by chunking material into pattern systems that it has used before. Learning is associated with increasing the patterns that students can use, recognize, and communicate. As the ability to see and work with patterns expands, and new material is presented in such a way that students see relationships, they can generate greater brain cell activity (i.e., formation of new neural connections) and achieve more successful patterns for long-term memory storage and retrieval.

plasticity (neuroplasticity): The brain's ability to change structurally and functionally as a result of learning and experience. This plasticity results in increased neuronal growth associated with repeated activation of a neural network. Dendrite formation and dendrite and neuron destruction (pruning) allow the brain to reshape and reorganize the networks of dendrite–neuron connections in response to increased or decreased use of these pathways.

positron emission tomography (PET): A neuroimaging technique that produces a three-dimensional image of functional processes in the body, based on the detection of radiation from the emission of positrons (tiny particles emitted from a radioactive substance administered to the subject in combination with glucose). As the subject engages in various cognitive activities, the scan records the rate at which specific regions of the brain use the glucose. These recordings are used to produce maps of areas of high brain activity with particular cognitive functions. The biggest drawback of PET scanning is that because the radioactivity decays rapidly, it is limited to monitoring short tasks. Newer fMRI technology does not have this same time limitation and has become the preferred functional imaging technique in learning research.

prefrontal cortex: The front part of the brain's frontal lobes. The prefrontal cortex is active in executive functions, long-term memories, and emotional control. It is associated with more reflective and cognitive information processing.

pruning: The process of destroying unused neurons. A baby's brain overproduces brain cells (neurons) and connections between brain cells (synapses) and then starts pruning them back around the age of 3. The second wave of synapse formation occurs just before puberty and is followed by another phase of pruning. Pruning allows the brain to consolidate learning by pruning away unused neurons and synapses and wrapping white matter (myelin) around the more frequently used neuronal networks to stabilize and strengthen them.

quantitative electroencephalography (qEEG): A technique that provides brain-mapping data based on the localization of brain wave patterns coming from the parts of the brain actively engaged in the processing of information. Quantitative EEG uses digital technology to record electrical patterns at the surface of the scalp that represent cortical electrical activity or brain waves. "Functional" qEEG testing adds recording to evaluate the brain's responses to reading, listening, calculating, or other demands to provide visual summaries in topographic maps.

reinforcement learning theories: Theories based on the assumption that the brain finds some states of stimulation to be more desirable than others and makes associations between specific cues and these desirable states or goals.

relational memory: A form of memory that takes place when students learn something that adds to what they have already mastered; the students engage or expand on "maps" already present in the brain.

reticular activating system (RAS): A lower part of the posterior brain that filters all incoming stimuli and edits what sensory information from the environment is admitted to the higher brain. The RAS alerts the brain to sensory input that sense receptors in the body send up the spinal cord. The main categories that focus the attention of the RAS include novelty and change, especially regarding possible threats or rewards.

rote memory: A type of memorization that is the most commonly required memory task for students in school. This type of learning involves memorizing, and usually forgetting, facts that are often of little primary interest or emotional value to the student, such as a list of words. Facts that are memorized by repeatedly rehearsing them, and that don't have obvious or engaging patterns or connections, are processed by rote memory. With nothing to give them context or relationship to one another—or to the students' lives—these facts are stored in more remote areas of the brain. These isolated bits are more difficult to locate and retrieve later because there are fewer nerve pathways leading to these remote storage systems.

serotonin: A neurotransmitter used to carry messages between neurons. Too little serotonin may be a cause of depression. Dendritic branching is enhanced by serotonin (as well as acetylcholine) secreted by the brain predominantly between the sixth and the eighth hour of sleep (non-REM).

somatosensory cortexes: Areas—one in each parietal brain lobe—where input from each sensory receptor (hearing, touch, taste, vision) is ultimately processed.

survival level of attention: The lowest level of attention needed to process and retain information. Too much stress can push students into survival mode, for example, when they feel confused and overwhelmed by a classroom experience to the degree that they cannot connect with, focus on, or create patterns and meaning from a lesson's sensory input data.

synapses: The specialized gaps between axons, dendrites, and neurons that are involved in information transfer. Neurotransmitters carry information across the space separating the axon extensions of one neuron from the dendrite that leads to the next neuron in the pathway. Before and after crossing the synapse as a chemical message, information is carried in an electrical state when it travels down the nerve.

temporal lobes: Lobes on the sides of the brain that process aspects of auditory and verbal input, spoken language, and mood stability through projection fibers leading to the limbic system.

thalamus: The part of the brain that processes sensory input and determines whether it will be kept in the temporary awareness portion of memory or be given more sustained attention. If it is processed as more than transient awareness, sensory input is passed through the thalamus to the neurons in the amygdala.

working memory: Short-term memory that can hold and manipulate information for use in the immediate future. Information is held in working memory for only about a minute.

zone of proximal development (ZPD): Lev Vygotsky's "zone of readiness," including the actions or topics a student is ready to learn. The zone of proximal development is the gap between a learner's current or actual level of development and his or her potential level of development. This is the set of knowledge that the learner does not yet understand but has the ability to learn with guidance.

References

AP-AOL News Poll. (2005, September 19). *The most unpopular school subject.* Available: http://diamondskyinc.com/research.asp?sid=3&cid=102&aid=73

Bender, W. (2005). *Differentiating math instruction.* Thousand Oaks, CA: Corwin Press.

Bishop, P., & Pflaum, S. (2005). Student perceptions of action, relevance, and pace. *Middle School Journal, 36*(4), 4–12.

Bransford, J., Brown, A. L., & Cocking, R. R. (Eds.). (2000). *How people learn: Brain, mind, experience, and school* (Expanded ed.). National Research Council, Committee on Learning Research and Educational Practice. Washington, DC: National Academies Press.

Britton, P. (2008). *Tutor training manual. AVID Region VIII curriculum guide.* San Diego, CA: AVID.

Brown, D. (2003). Urban teachers' use of culturally responsive management strategies. *Theory into Practice, 42*(4), 277–282.

Comer, J. (1993). *School power: Implications of an intervention project.* New York: Free Press.

Cordova, D. I., & Lepper, M. R. (1996). Intrinsic motivation and the process of learning: Beneficial effects of contextualization, personalization, and choice. *Journal of Educational Psychology, 88*(4), 715–730.

Crone, E. A., Donohue, S. E., Honomichl, R., Wendelken, C., & Bunge, S. A. (2006). Brain regions mediating flexible rule use during development. *The Journal of Neuroscience, 26*(43), 11239–11247.

Csikszentmihalyi, M. (1991). *Flow: The psychology of optimal experience.* New York: HarperColllins.

Din, F. S., & Calao, J. (2001). The effects of playing educational video games on kindergarten achievement. *Child Study Journal, 31*(2), 95–102.

Duckworth, A., & Seligman, M. (2005). Self-discipline outdoes IQ in predicting academic performance of adolescents. *Psychological Science, 16*(12), 939–944.

Dweck, C. (2000). *Self-theories: Their role in motivation, personality, and development.* New York: Psychology Press.

Ericsson, K. A. (1996). The acquisition of expert performance: An introduction to some of the issues. In K. A. Ericsson (Ed.), *The road to excellence: The acquisition of expert performance in the arts and sciences, sports and games* (pp. 1–50). Mahwah, NJ: Lawrence Erlbaum Associates.

Eriksen, C., & Schultz, D. (1979). Information processing in visual search: A continuous flow conception and experimental results. *Perception and Psychophysics, 25*(4), 249–263.

Fredrickson, B. L., Tugade, M. M., Waugh, C. E., & Larkin, G. (2003). What good are positive emotions? A prospective study of resilience and emotions. *Journal of Personality and Social Psychology, 84*(2), 365–376.

Gardner, H. (1983). *Frames of mind: The theory of multiple intelligences.* New York: Basic Books.

Gardner, H. (2000). *Intelligence reframed: Multiple intelligences for the 21st century.* New York: BasicBooks.

Gee, J. P. (2003). *What video games have to teach us about learning and literacy.* New York: Palgrave Macmillan.

Goleman, D. (1995). *Emotional intelligence.* New York: Bantam.

Guthrie, J. T., & Wigfield, A. (2000). Engagement and motivation in reading. In M. L. Kamil, P. B. Mosenthal, P. D. Pearson, & R. Barr (Eds.), *Handbook of reading research: Volume III* (pp. 403–422). New York: Lawrence Erlbaum Associates.

Harris, S. (1977). *What's so funny about science? Cartoons from American Scientist.* New York: William Kaufmann.

Hembree, R., & Dessart, D. J. (1986). Effects of hand-held calculators in precollege mathematics education: A meta-analysis. *Journal for Research in Mathematics Education, 17*(2), 83–99.

Hillman, C., Pontifex, M., Raine, L., Castelli, D., Hall, E., & Kramer, A. (2009). The effect of acute treadmill walking on cognitive control and academic achievement in preadolescent children. *Neuroscience, 159*(3), 1044–1054.

Hopko, D., Ashcraft, M., & Gute, J. (1998). Mathematics anxiety and working memory: Support for the existence of a deficient inhibition mechanism. *Journal of Anxiety Disorders, 12*(4), 343–355.

Hunkin, N. M., Mayes, A. R., Gregory, L. J., Nicholas, A. K., Nunn, J. A., Brammer, M. J., Bullmore, E. T., & Williams, S. C. R. (2002). Novelty-related activation within the medial temporal lobes. *Neuropsychologia, 40*(8), 1456–1464.

Kienast, T., Hariri, A., Schlagenhauf, F., Wrase, J., Sterzer, P., Buchholz, H., Smolka, M., Gründer, G., Cumming, P., Kumakura, Y., Bartenstein, P., Dolan, R., & Heinz, A. (2008). Dopamine in amygdala gates limbic processing of aversive stimuli in humans. *Nature Neuroscience, 11*(12), 1381–1382.

Kinomura, L., Larsson, J., Gulyas, A., & Roland, L. (1996). Activation by attention of the human reticular formation and thalamic intralaminar nuclei. *Science, 271*(5248), 512–514.

Lawrence, N. S., Ross, T. J., Hoffman, R., Garavan, H., & Stein, E. A. (2003). Multiple neuronal networks mediate sustained attention. *Journal of Cognitive Neuroscience, 15*(7), 1028–1038.

LeDoux, J. (1994). Emotion, memory and the brain. *Scientific American, 270*(6), 50–57.

Li, S., Cullen, W. K., Anwyl, R., & Rowan, M. J. (2003). Dopamine-dependent facilitation of LTP induction in hippocampal CA1 by exposure to spatial novelty. *Nature Neuroscience, 6*(5), 526–531.

Malone, T. (1982). What makes computer games fun? *ACM SIGSOC, 13*(2–3), 143.

McCandliss, B. D., Cohen, L., & Dehaene, S. (2003). The visual word form area: Expertise for reading in the fusiform gyrus. *Trends in Cognitive Sciences, 7*(7), 293–299.

Merabet, L. B., Hamilton, R., Schlaug, G., Swisher, J. D., Kiriakopoulos, E. T., Pitskel, N. B., Kauffman, T., & Pascual-Leone, A. (2008). Rapid and reversible recruitment of early visual cortex for touch. *PLoS ONE, 3*(8), 3046–3049.

Mischel, W., Shoda, Y., & Rodriguez, M. (1989). Delay of gratification in children. *Science, 244*(4907), 407–413.

Neild, R., Balfanz, R., & Herzog, L. (2007). Early intervention at every age. *Educational Leadership, 65*(2), 28–33.

Organization for Economic Co-operation and Development. (2004, August). *Policy brief: Internationalisation of higher education.* Available: http://www.oecd.org/dataoecd/33/60/33734276.pdf

Palmer, B., Codling, R., & Gambrel, L. (1994). In their own words: What elementary students have to say about motivation to read. *The Reading Teacher, 48*(2), 176–178.

Phillips, G. W. (2007). *Chance favors the prepared mind: Mathematics and science indicators for comparing states and nations.* Washington, DC: American Institutes for Research.

Sethi, A., Mischel, W., Aber, J. L., Shoda, Y., & Rodriguez, M. L. (2000). The role of strategic attention deployment in development of self-regulation: Predicting preschoolers' delay of gratification from mother-toddler interactions. *Developmental Psychology, 36*(6), 767–777.

Shoda, Y., Mischel, W., & Peake, P. K. (1990). Predicting adolescent cognitive and self-regulatory competencies from preschool delay of gratification: Identifying diagnostic conditions. *Developmental Psychology, 26*(6), 978–986.

Subramaniam, K., Kounios, J., Bowden, E., Parrish, T., & Jung-Beeman, M. (2009). Positive mood and anxiety modulate anterior cingulate activity and cognitive preparation for insight. *Journal of Cognitive Neuroscience, 21,* 415–432.

U.S. Department of Education. (2008). *The final report of the National Mathematics Advisory Council.* Washington, DC: Education Publications Center, U.S. Department of Education. Available: http://www2.ed.gov/about/bdscomm/list/mathpanel/report/final-report.pdf

Van Duijvenvoorde, A., Zanolie, K., Rombouts, S., Raijmakers, M., & Crone, E. (2008). Evaluating the negative or valuing the positive? Neural mechanisms supporting feedback-based learning across development. *The Journal of Neuroscience, 28*(38), 9495–9503.

Van Overwalle, F., & De Metsenaere, M. (1990). The effects of attribution-based intervention and study strategy training on academic achievement in college freshmen. *British Journal of Educational Psychology, 60*(3), 299–311.

Vigneua, F., Caissie, A., & Bors, D. (2006). Eye-movement analysis demonstrates strategic influences on intelligence. *Intelligence, 34*(3), 261–272.

Walker, H., Colvin, G., & Ramsey, E. (1995). *Antisocial behavior in school: Strategies and best practices.* Pacific Grove, CA: Brooks/Cole.

Wang, J., Rao, H., & Wetmoree, G. (2005). Perfusion functional MRI reveals cerebral blood flow pattern under psychological stress. *Proceedings of the National Academy of Sciences, 102*(49), 17804–17809.

Yazzie-Mintz, E. (2007). *Voices of students on engagement: A report on the 2006 High School Survey of Student Engagement.* Bloomington, IN: Center for Evaluation & Education Policy, Indiana University. Retrieved April 16, 2008, from http://ceep.indiana.edu/hssse/pdf/HSSSE_2006_Report.pdf

Index

About the Author

After graduating Phi Beta Kappa as the first woman graduate from Williams College, Judy Willis attended UCLA School of Medicine where she was awarded her medical degree. She remained at UCLA and completed a medical residency and neurology residency, including chief residency. She practiced neurology for 15 years before returning to university to obtain her teaching credential and master's of education from the University of California, Santa Barbara. She has taught in elementary and middle school for the past 10 years.

Dr. Willis is an authority on brain research regarding learning and the brain. She writes extensively for professional educational journals and has written six books about applying the mind, brain, and education research to classroom teaching strategies. The Association of Educational Publishers honored Dr. Willis as a 2007 finalist for the Distinguished Achievement Award for her educational writing.

Dr. Willis is a presenter at educational conferences and conducts professional development workshops nationally and internationally about classroom strategies correlated with neuroscience research, and she has been a Distinguished and Featured Presenter at ASCD national conferences. Her books include *Research-Based Strategies to Ignite Student Learning, Brain-Friendly Strategies for the Inclusion Classroom, Teaching the Brain to Read, Inspiring Middle School Minds,* and *How Your Child Learns Best.*

A research consultant and member of the board of directors for the Hawn Foundation, Dr. Willis cowrote the curriculum for teachers to use to implement mindful educational programs in their classrooms. In 2010, Dr. Willis was recognized by the American Academy of Neurology for her work to increase educator access to the neuroscience research applicable to learning. Her contributions were featured in the cover story of their journal, *Neurology Now.*

When not teaching, writing, consulting, or presenting, Dr. Willis is a home winemaker and writes a weekly wine column. You can contact her at jwillisneuro@aol.com or visit her Web site at www.RADTeach.com.

Related ASCD Resources

At the time of publication, the following ASCD resources were available (ASCD stock numbers appear in parentheses). For up-to-date information about ASCD resources, go to www.ascd.org. You can search the complete archives of *Educational Leadership* at http://www.ascd.org/el.

Networks

Visit the ASCD Web site (www.ascd.org) and search for "networks" for information about professional educators who have formed groups around topics like "Assessment for Learning," "Brain-Compatible Learning," and "Quality Education." Look in the "Network Directory" for current facilitators' addresses and phone numbers.

Print Products

The Brain-Compatible Classroom: Using What We Know About Learning to Improve Teaching by Laura Erlauer (#101269)

Brain Matters: Translating Research into Classroom Practice (2nd edition) by Patricia Wolfe (#109073)

Concept-Rich Mathematics Instruction: Building a Strong Foundation for Reasoning and Problem Solving by Meir Ben-Hur (#106008)

The Essentials of Mathematics, K–6: Effective Curriculum, Instruction, and Assessment by Kathy Checkley (#106032)

Literacy Strategies for Improving Mathematics Instruction by Joan M. Kenney, Euthecia Hancewicz, Loretta Heuer, Diana Metsisto, and Cynthia L. Tuttle (#105137)

The Motivated Student: Unlocking the Enthusiasm for Learning by Bob Sullo (#109028)

Research-Based Strategies to Ignite Student Learning by Judy Willis (#107006)

Videos

The Brain and Mathematics (#600237)

Meaningful Mathematics: Leading Students Toward Understanding and Application (#607085)

Teaching the Adolescent Brain (#606050)

WHOLE CHILD The Whole Child Initiative helps schools and communities create learning environments that allow students to be healthy, safe, engaged, supported, and challenged. To learn more about other books and resources that relate to the whole child, visit www.wholechildeducation.org.

For more information: send e-mail to member@ascd.org; call 1-800-933-2723 or 703-578-9600, press 2; send a fax to 703-575-5400; or write to Information Services, ASCD, 1703 N. Beauregard St., Alexandria, VA 22311-1714 USA.